EL SALVA
TRAVEL GUIDE
2025

Discover El Salvador's Accommodations, tourist attractions and spots. Practical Tips and Local Insights

Julienne Lemelin

All rights reserved. No part of this book may be reproduced, stored in a retrieval system, or transmitted in any form or by any means, electronic, mechanical, photocopying, recording, or otherwise, without the prior written permission of the copyright owner. The information contained in this book is for general information purposes only. The author and publisher make no representations or warranties of any kind, express or implied, about the completeness, accuracy, reliability, suitability or availability with respect to the book or the information, products, services, or related graphics contained in the book for any purpose. Any reliance you place on such information is therefore strictly at your own risk.

Copyright © 2025 by Julienne Lemelin

Table of Contents

Introduction 5
    History & Customs 5
Chapter 1: Planning Your Trip 9
    Time to visit 9
    Visa and Entry Requirements 13
    What to pack 16
    Neighborhoods to Stay in El Salvador 20
    Hotels in El Salvador: A Comfortable Stay Awaits 32
    Hostels in El Salvador 43
Chapter 2: Tourist Attractions & Spots in El Salvador 53
Chapter 3: Gastronomic Delight & Entertainment 64
    Local Dishes to Try Out in El Salvador 64
    Local Drinks to Try Out in El Salvador 70
    Restaurants in El Salvador: A Culinary Adventure Through Local and International Flavors 75
    Street Food in El Salvador: A Gastronomic Adventure You Can't Miss 86
    Food Markets in El Salvador: A Journey Through Flavor and Culture 97
    Bars and Pubs in El Salvador 108
    Nightclubs in El Salvador: Where to Dance the Night Away 119
Chapter 4: Travel Itineraries 129

Outdoor Adventure Itinerary in El Salvador: From Volcanoes to Beaches 129

Romantic Itinerary 134

Discovering El Salvador's Coastline: A Personal Journey of Sun, Surf, and Serenity 137

Budget-Friendly Itinerary in El Salvador: A Personal Journey 141

Exploring El Salvador's Historical Wonders: A Journey Through Time 147

Family-Friendly Itinerary in El Salvador: A Personal Experience 152

Chapter 5: Cultural Experiences 158

Festivals in El Salvador: A Cultural Celebration of Vibrancy and Tradition 158

Exploring the Rich Tapestry of Museums and Galleries in El Salvador 169

Off-the-Beaten-Path Attractions in El Salvador 179

Chapter 6: Practical Information 190

Safety and Security Considerations 190

Money Matters and Currency Exchange 193

Health Precautions 197

Emergency Contact Numbers in El Salvador: A Traveler's Guide with Personal Insights 202

Transportation & Getting Around in El Salvador: A Personal Guide 207

INTRODUCTION

History & Customs

El Salvador's history and customs are like a rich tapestry, interwoven with vibrant threads of resilience, tradition, and cultural pride. Imagine walking through the streets of San Salvador or the quaint cobblestone towns like Suchitoto, and you'll feel an undeniable pulse—a heartbeat that reflects the struggles and celebrations of this small yet profoundly impactful nation. This journey into El Salvador's story is not just about dates and events; it's about the soul of its people, their indomitable spirit, and the traditions they hold close.

The history of El Salvador, or as locals affectionately call it, *El Pulgarcito de América* (The Little Thumb of America), begins long before the Spanish arrived. Indigenous groups, notably the Pipil people, left their mark on the land with their unique language, Nahuatl, and advanced agricultural systems. The Pipil were descendants of the Toltecs and Aztecs, and their legacy is visible in the ruins of places like Joya de Cerén, often called the "Pompeii of the Americas." Visiting these archaeological sites, you can almost hear the whispers of ancient life—the bustling markets, the planting of maize, the rituals to honor their gods. It's humbling to stand where these civilizations thrived, feeling connected to an era where community and harmony with nature were central.

Spanish colonization, as with much of Latin America, brought profound changes. The land was named after Jesus Christ—"El Salvador," meaning "The Savior." Yet, the savior's name belied the harsh realities that followed. Indigenous populations were decimated by disease and forced labor, and the Spanish reshaped society to revolve around the *encomienda* system. This era marked the beginning of a sharp divide between the landowning elites and the laboring classes, a division that would define El Salvador's social fabric for centuries.

Walking through the grand colonial churches, like the Metropolitan Cathedral of San Salvador or the Church of El Rosario, you can feel the weight of this history. These structures, with their intricate facades and serene interiors, stand as testaments to the influence of Catholicism. But religion in El Salvador is not confined to ornate buildings; it spills into the streets, especially during holy festivals. Semana Santa, or Holy Week, is a spectacle to behold. I remember watching the processions, where locals carried elaborately decorated floats of the Virgin Mary and Christ through the streets, accompanied by somber music and the scent of incense. It's not just a religious event—it's a deeply emotional experience that unites communities in devotion.

Fast forward to the 20th century, and El Salvador's history takes a turbulent turn. The country's beauty is matched only by the resilience of its people, who endured a brutal civil war from 1980 to 1992. Visiting the Monument to Memory and Truth in San Salvador was a sobering experience. The names of thousands of victims etched into the walls speak volumes about the pain and loss endured by so many families. Yet, amidst the sorrow, there's a spirit of perseverance. Salvadorans carry their history not as a burden but as a badge of honor, a reminder of their capacity to rebuild and hope.

El Salvador's customs and traditions are where the light shines brightest. One of the most heartwarming aspects of Salvadoran culture is its emphasis on family. Every meal, every celebration, every Sunday gathering revolves around the idea of togetherness. Pupusas, the national dish, are more than just food—they're a symbol of Salvadoran identity. Watching a local woman skillfully pat dough filled with cheese, beans, or pork before grilling it on a comal is mesmerizing. The smell alone transports you to a place of comfort. And when you sit down to eat, surrounded by laughter and chatter, it's impossible not to feel a part of something larger.

Festivals in El Salvador are colorful, lively, and deeply rooted in tradition. One unforgettable experience is the *Fiesta de las Flores y Palmas* in Panchimalco. This centuries-old celebration involves processions of people adorned with vibrant flowers, honoring the Virgin Mary. It's a sensory overload—the vibrant colors of the flowers, the rhythmic drumming, and the palpable joy of the participants create an atmosphere that's almost magical. Similarly, the *Bolas de Fuego* festival in Nejapa is an adrenaline-pumping event where participants throw fireballs at each other, reenacting a legendary volcanic eruption. It's wild and chaotic, but it's also a reminder of the Salvadoran spirit—fearless and full of life.

Music and dance are lifelines of Salvadoran customs. The rhythmic beats of cumbia and salsa are infectious, and you'll often see people spontaneously breaking into dance during local festivities. One night in El Salvador, I found myself in a small town square where a band was playing traditional folk music. Couples danced gracefully, their movements a blend of tradition and passion. It was impossible not to join in, and even though my steps were clumsy, the locals welcomed me with open arms, laughing and teaching me their moves.

The Salvadoran people have a unique way of blending the old with the new. While modernization is evident in cities like San Salvador, where malls and skyscrapers dominate the skyline, the heart of the culture remains rooted in its traditions. The bustling markets, like the one in Santa Ana, are perfect examples of this. Vendors sell everything from handmade crafts to fresh produce, their stalls brimming with the vibrant energy of daily life. It's here that you can truly appreciate the art of Salvadoran craftsmanship— intricately woven textiles, pottery, and jewelry that tell stories of the past while remaining relevant in the present.

Another remarkable custom is the Salvadoran love for storytelling. Sitting around a fire, elders recount tales of *La Siguanaba* or *El Cipitío*, mythical figures that are both cautionary and entertaining. These stories are more than just folklore; they're a way of preserving the past and passing on lessons to younger generations. Listening to these tales under a starlit sky, you can't help but feel connected to something timeless.

What struck me most about El Salvador is its people. Despite a history marked by hardship, Salvadorans exude warmth and kindness. They greet strangers with a genuine smile, eager to share their stories and culture. I remember meeting a local farmer who proudly showed me his coffee plantation. Over a cup of freshly brewed coffee, he spoke about his family's struggles and triumphs, his words laced with a sense of pride and hope for the future. Moments like these are what make El Salvador unforgettable.

As I wandered through the country, from the volcanic landscapes of Cerro Verde to the serene beaches of El Tunco, I realized that El Salvador's history and customs are not just about the past—they're a living, breathing part of everyday life. Every tradition, every story, every meal is a testament to the resilience and creativity of its people. El Salvador may be small, but its heart is immense, and its culture leaves an indelible mark on anyone fortunate enough to experience it.

CHAPTER 1: PLANNING YOUR TRIP

Time to visit

Visiting El Salvador feels like uncovering a gem that has been waiting for you all along. Deciding when to visit this beautiful Central American country can be tricky because every season brings something special. I remember how I debated for days before booking my trip, sifting through advice from locals and fellow travelers. The thing about El Salvador is that its charm isn't limited to one perfect season. It depends on what you're looking for—whether it's lush greenery, thrilling waves, or the buzz of cultural festivities.

When I first arrived, it was during the dry season, which runs from November to April. Some call it the best time to visit, and I understand why. The skies were clear, the weather was warm but not stifling, and exploring the landscapes was a breeze. I spent days wandering through national parks, trekking up volcanoes like Santa Ana, and marveling at Lake Coatepeque's shimmering waters. It was during this time that I realized how easy it is to fall in love with El Salvador. The roads are more accessible during the dry season, which is great if you plan to rent a car and explore. Trust me, you'll want to drive along the Ruta de Las Flores, a scenic route dotted with charming villages, vibrant murals, and aromatic coffee farms.

For surfers, the dry season is paradise. I remember sitting on El Tunco beach, watching surfers tackle waves that seemed almost too perfect to be real. El Salvador is famous for its surf spots, and places like Punta Roca and El Zonte become magnets for wave chasers. Even if you're not into surfing, there's something magical about the vibe here. The sunsets were spectacular; I'd sit with my toes in the sand, sipping on a cold Suprema beer, watching the sky explode into shades of pink and orange. It's the kind of moment that makes you pause and appreciate how simple and beautiful life can be.

That being said, the rainy season, which spans from May to October, has its own allure. I've been told that this is when El Salvador truly comes alive with vibrant greenery and the scent of fresh rain lingering in the air. Some people shy away from visiting during this time because they worry about heavy downpours, but honestly, it's not as bad as you might think. The rain usually comes in the late afternoon or evening, leaving the mornings bright and sunny. If you're into photography or nature, this is the time to come. The landscapes are stunning—waterfalls gush with newfound energy, and the coffee plantations look like they belong in a postcard.

One of the highlights of the rainy season is how peaceful it can be. The tourist crowds thin out, which means you get to enjoy popular spots without feeling rushed or cramped. I remember walking through the ruins of Joya de Cerén, often called the "Pompeii of the Americas," and feeling like I had the entire site to myself. It's a UNESCO World Heritage Site, and being there with fewer visitors made the experience feel even more special. There's something humbling about standing in a place frozen in time, where the remnants of an ancient Mayan village tell stories of a world long gone.

If you're lucky enough to visit during the transition between seasons, you'll get the best of both worlds. I once planned a trip in late October, and it was magical. The rains were tapering off, but the landscapes still had that lush, vibrant quality. The air felt fresh, and the temperatures were just right. Plus, this is when you start to see preparations for festivals and holidays, which add an extra layer of excitement to your trip.

One festival that left a lasting impression on me was the Day of the Dead, or Día de los Muertos. It's celebrated in early November, and while it's not as grand as in Mexico, it has its own unique charm in El Salvador. I joined a local family as they decorated graves with flowers, candles, and food offerings. It was a deeply moving experience, filled with warmth and a sense of connection to something greater. If you ever have the chance to visit during this time, I highly recommend it. It's moments like these that remind you of the richness of Salvadoran culture.

Of course, weather isn't the only factor to consider when planning your trip. If you're a coffee lover like me, you might want to time your visit with the coffee harvest season, which typically runs from November to February. El Salvador is renowned for its coffee, and touring a plantation during harvest season is an experience like no other. I remember sipping on freshly brewed coffee at a farm in the Apaneca-Ilamatepec region, feeling the crisp mountain air and marveling at the rows of coffee plants stretching out before me. It was one of those moments that stays with you long after you've left.

Another thing to keep in mind is that El Salvador has microclimates, so the weather can vary depending on where you go. The coastal areas are generally warmer, while the highlands offer cooler, more temperate conditions. I learned this the hard way when I packed only for beach weather and found myself shivering on a chilly evening in Suchitoto, a picturesque colonial town. Speaking of Suchitoto, this place is a must-visit regardless of the season. Its cobblestone streets, colorful buildings, and art galleries make it feel like stepping back in time. If you're lucky, you might catch a local festival or artisan market during your visit.

Traveling during the peak season, which coincides with the dry months and major holidays like Christmas and Easter, can be both exciting and challenging. I remember visiting during Semana Santa (Holy Week) and being blown away by the elaborate processions and celebrations. The streets were alive with music, incense, and vibrant carpets made of colored sawdust and flowers. It's a beautiful time to experience Salvadoran traditions, but it's also when popular destinations can get crowded. If you're planning to visit during this time, I'd recommend booking accommodations well in advance.

On the flip side, the low season offers a different kind of magic. With fewer tourists around, you'll find that locals have more time to share their stories and recommendations. Some of my favorite memories come from chatting with shopkeepers, guides, and café owners who were genuinely excited to share the best of their country with me. This is also when you're more likely to score deals on accommodations and tours, which is always a bonus.

In the end, there's no wrong time to visit El Salvador. Each season has its own unique appeal, and the best time for you will depend on what you want to experience. Whether it's the golden days of the dry season, the lush beauty of the rainy months, or the cultural vibrancy of festival periods, El Salvador has a way of captivating your heart no matter when you go. So pack your bags, keep an open mind, and get ready for an adventure that's bound to stay with you long after you've left this incredible country.

Visa and Entry Requirements

Traveling to El Salvador is a vibrant adventure, and understanding the visa and entry requirements is one of the first steps to making your journey as seamless as possible. I remember the first time I planned my trip there, I had a mix of excitement and a bit of anxiety over whether I had all my paperwork in order. Let me walk you through what you need, just like a friend who's been through it and wants to share all the insider tips.

For most travelers, the good news is that El Salvador has a relatively straightforward process for entry. If you're coming from many countries, including the United States, Canada, and most of Europe, you don't need a visa for short stays. You're allowed to stay for up to 90 days on just a passport and a tourist card. Now, here's a tip: that tourist card is something you purchase upon arrival. It costs around $12, and you'll typically pay for it at immigration before they stamp your passport. It's a small detail, but I can tell you it saves a lot of hassle to have some cash in US dollars ready for this.

Speaking of passports, make sure yours is valid for at least six months beyond your planned departure date. This is one of those rules that can easily slip your mind, but it's crucial. I once met a fellow traveler at the airport who had to reschedule their entire trip because their passport didn't meet the six-month requirement. It's a small detail that can make or break your plans.

Now, if you're someone who isn't from a visa-exempt country, don't worry—it's not too complicated. You'll need to apply for a visa in advance at an El Salvadoran consulate or embassy. The process usually involves filling out an application form, providing a passport-sized photo, proof of travel plans, and sometimes financial documentation. It's not as daunting as it sounds, but it's always a good idea to start the application process early, just in case there are any hiccups. I always say, when it comes to travel, preparation is your best friend.

For those planning longer stays, maybe for work, study, or extended travel, the requirements change a bit. You'll need a different type of visa, and the process is more detailed. For example, if you're applying for a work visa, your employer in El Salvador will likely play a role in the application process, providing necessary documents like a job offer letter. It's best to get in touch with the consulate or embassy to understand the specific requirements for your situation. I've heard from friends who've gone through this that while it takes some patience, the officials are generally helpful and will guide you through what's needed.

One thing that stood out to me during my trip planning was how El Salvador is part of the CA-4 agreement with Guatemala, Honduras, and Nicaragua. This means that once you're in one of these countries, you can travel between them without needing another visa within the 90-day period. It's perfect if you're planning a multi-country adventure in Central America. I took full advantage of this when I was there, hopping over to Guatemala and Honduras without any additional paperwork. It felt like a bonus perk of visiting this region.

Let's talk about customs and immigration at the airport. When you arrive in El Salvador, the process is usually pretty straightforward. You'll need to fill out an immigration form on the plane or upon arrival, detailing your travel plans and where you'll be staying. Having the address of your hotel or accommodation handy is a must—I learned that the hard way when I had to dig through my phone at the counter. If you're staying with friends or family, their address will work too. The immigration officers are generally friendly, but having your information organized helps speed up the process.

Another thing to keep in mind is the yellow fever vaccine requirement. If you're traveling from a country where yellow fever is endemic, you'll need to show proof of vaccination. It's not something everyone needs, but if it applies to you, it's better to be safe than sorry. I didn't need it for my trip, but I met a traveler from Brazil who was glad they had their vaccine certificate handy.

And let's not forget about the departure process. When you're leaving El Salvador, you'll usually pay an exit tax, which is sometimes included in your airfare. If it's not included, you'll need to pay it at the airport before you can board your flight. It's another reason to have some cash on hand—preferably US dollars, as they're widely accepted and actually the official currency in El Salvador. I always make it a point to double-check my flight details and taxes ahead of time to avoid any surprises.

For digital nomads or long-term travelers, the situation can be a bit more nuanced. If you're thinking of extending your stay beyond the initial 90 days, you'll need to apply for an extension or leave the CA-4 region and return to reset your visa period. I've met a few expats who make a quick trip to Costa Rica or Mexico before coming back to El Salvador. It's a bit of a workaround, but it's fairly common and totally doable.

If there's one piece of advice I'd emphasize, it's to double-check the latest travel advisories and entry requirements before your trip. Rules can change, and what applied a year ago might not be the case now. When I planned my trip, I made sure to visit the official website of El Salvador's consulate and even called them to confirm the details. It gave me peace of mind knowing I had the most accurate information.

Also, keep copies of your important documents, like your passport, visa (if applicable), and travel insurance, both digitally and in print. I learned this habit from a seasoned traveler I met years ago, and it's saved me more than once. In El Salvador, I felt safe and welcomed, but having backups of everything just made me feel that much more secure.

All in all, the process of getting into El Salvador is smooth for most travelers. With a bit of preparation and attention to detail, you'll be ready to dive into the country's incredible beaches, lush landscapes, and vibrant culture without any unnecessary stress. Trust me, the effort is worth it—El Salvador is a destination that stays with you long after you've left.

What to pack

Packing for a trip to El Salvador is all about finding that balance between practicality and comfort. This is a country that offers a mix of vibrant cities, lush mountains, sunny beaches, and a warm climate, so it's essential to think about what you'll need to stay comfortable while also respecting the local culture. When I prepared for my own adventure in El Salvador, I learned a lot about what to bring—and more importantly, what not to bring. Let me walk you through it, so you can avoid the guesswork.

First off, lightweight clothing is an absolute must. El Salvador's tropical climate means it's warm to hot year-round, so think breathable fabrics like cotton and linen. I remember stepping off the plane and immediately being thankful I wore a loose, airy outfit for the flight. T-shirts, tank tops, and light dresses were my go-to pieces during the day. Shorts are fine for casual outings, especially at the beach, but I also packed a couple of light pants for hiking or when I wanted to be more covered up, like when visiting certain areas where shorts felt a little too casual.

Speaking of coverage, something I didn't fully appreciate before my trip was how important it is to dress respectfully in certain places. While the beach towns like El Tunco are super laid-back and anything goes, when you're exploring cities like San Salvador or small rural villages, modest clothing is appreciated. That's where those light pants or longer skirts came in handy. I always felt comfortable and like I was blending in more with the locals when I was a bit more conservative in my outfit choices.

Now, let's talk footwear. This is where I got it both right and wrong on my first trip. For the beach, flip-flops or sandals are perfect—I lived in mine while exploring coastal areas. But I quickly learned that sturdy, comfortable walking shoes or lightweight hiking boots are essential if you plan to do any exploring beyond the beach. I brought a pair of sneakers that worked fine for city walking, but when I went hiking in the Ruta de las Flores or exploring waterfalls, I wished I had something with better grip and ankle support. Trust me, the terrain can be uneven and slippery, so don't underestimate the importance of good shoes.

Don't forget a swimsuit—or maybe even two. Whether you're planning to surf in El Tunco, relax at a lakeside retreat like Lago de Coatepeque, or cool off in a waterfall, you'll want swimwear that's comfortable and versatile. I brought one sporty swimsuit for more active days and another for lounging, and it worked out perfectly. Oh, and a quick-dry towel is a lifesaver—it packs small and is super convenient for beach days or even spontaneous swims when you're hiking.

One thing I'm so glad I didn't overlook was a lightweight jacket or sweater. Yes, it's warm in El Salvador, but nights in the mountains or on higher-altitude hikes can get surprisingly chilly. I remember one evening in the charming town of Ataco—I was sitting outside, enjoying a cup of local coffee, and the temperature dropped significantly once the sun went down. A light jacket made all the difference.

A rain jacket or a compact travel umbrella is another item that might not seem obvious at first but is worth having, especially if you're visiting during the rainy season, which typically runs from May to October. The rain showers often come in the late afternoon and can be heavy but brief. I learned the hard way after getting caught in a sudden downpour in Suchitoto without any protection. Now, I always tuck a small, packable raincoat into my daypack.

Let's talk about essentials for the strong Salvadoran sun. Sunscreen is non-negotiable—it's something you'll want to apply daily, even if you're just walking around town. A wide-brimmed hat or a good baseball cap was a lifesaver for me, especially during long days of exploring ruins like Joya de Cerén or wandering through open markets. Sunglasses with UV protection are another must; I'd say they're just as important as sunscreen in keeping you comfortable.

Bug spray is another item you won't want to leave behind. Mosquitoes can be pesky, especially in more humid areas or if you're near water. I made sure to pack a good DEET-based repellent, and I also brought along some anti-itch cream just in case. It's one of those things you hope you won't need but will be so glad to have if you do.

For toiletries, keep it simple but thorough. You'll want travel-sized versions of all your basics, but don't forget things like a good quality shampoo and conditioner if you're planning to spend a lot of time in the sun or saltwater—your hair will thank you. If you wear makeup, consider going minimal; the heat and humidity can make it challenging to keep a full face intact. A tinted moisturizer with SPF was all I used most days.

One thing that surprised me was how much I relied on a reusable water bottle. Staying hydrated is key, especially if you're not used to the heat. Many hotels and hostels have filtered water available, so having a bottle you can refill not only saves money but also reduces plastic waste. I also packed some electrolyte tablets—they came in handy after long days of exploring under the sun.

For tech and gadgets, you don't need much, but the right items can make your trip smoother. A portable charger was a game-changer for me; between taking photos, navigating with maps, and looking up recommendations, my phone was always in use. I also brought a universal power adapter, as El Salvador uses the same outlets as the U.S., but it's always good to be prepared if you're coming from somewhere else.

One thing I underestimated was how much I'd use a small daypack. I initially thought my regular travel bag would be enough, but having something lightweight and compact for daily outings made life so much easier. It's perfect for carrying essentials like water, sunscreen, snacks, and a camera without being too bulky.

Speaking of snacks, it's always a good idea to pack a few. While El Salvador's food is incredible and you'll find plenty of pupusas and fresh fruits to keep you satisfied, having a few energy bars or trail mix packets is helpful for hikes or long travel days. I especially appreciated them on bus rides when I didn't know when the next food stop would be.

Lastly, don't forget the little things that can make a big difference. A travel-size first-aid kit with band-aids, antiseptic wipes, and any personal medications is essential. I also threw in some motion sickness tablets, which came in handy on winding mountain roads. A small notebook or journal is great for jotting down memories or keeping track of recommendations from locals—I always find it adds a nice personal touch to the experience.

When it comes to money, cash is king in many parts of El Salvador, so bring some U.S. dollars in small denominations, as it's the official currency. ATMs are available in cities, but it's good to have cash on hand for rural areas or markets. Just make sure you have a secure way to carry it, like a money belt or hidden pouch.

Overall, packing for El Salvador isn't complicated, but it does require a bit of thought about the variety of experiences you'll have. From the vibrant streets of San Salvador to the laid-back vibes of the beaches and the stunning natural beauty of the national parks, having the right gear made my trip so much more enjoyable. If you keep it light, versatile, and practical, you'll be ready to enjoy everything this beautiful country has to offer.

Neighborhoods to Stay in El Salvador

If you're planning a trip to El Salvador, you're in for a treat. This small but vibrant Central American country has a lot to offer, from stunning beaches to picturesque mountain towns. One of the most important decisions you'll make is where to stay, as your choice of neighborhood can greatly influence your experience. Having spent time exploring El Salvador, I can confidently guide you through some of the best neighborhoods to consider based on what you're looking for.

1. San Benito (San Salvador)

For a Modern, Upscale Experience

When I first arrived in San Salvador, I was struck by the contrast between the bustling city and the calm, modern vibe of San Benito. This neighborhood is a hub for business travelers and expats, but it also has plenty to offer tourists. It's clean, safe, and dotted with trendy cafes, art galleries, and some of the city's best restaurants.

- **What to Expect**: San Benito feels like the heartbeat of modern San Salvador. The streets are lined with embassies, boutique hotels, and stylish coworking spaces.

- **Why I Recommend It**: I loved staying here because it felt like a little oasis amid the hustle and bustle of the capital. After a day of exploring the city's historical landmarks, coming back to this peaceful neighborhood was such a relief.
- **Highlights**: The Museo de Arte de El Salvador (MARTE) is right in the area and offers an incredible glimpse into Salvadoran culture. Don't miss dinner at La Gastroteca, one of my favorite restaurants for a fusion of local and international flavors.

2. El Tunco (La Libertad)

For Beach Lovers and Surfers

El Tunco is where my love for El Salvador's beach culture blossomed. Known internationally as a surfing hotspot, this small coastal town exudes a laid-back, bohemian vibe. Whether you're a pro surfer or someone who just wants to dip their toes in the ocean, this is the place to be.

- **What to Expect**: The main strip is filled with surf shops, casual bars, and eateries serving fresh seafood. Don't expect luxury here – it's more about the barefoot, carefree lifestyle.
- **Why I Recommend It**: Waking up to the sound of waves crashing against the shore is unbeatable. I spent my mornings sipping coffee at a beachfront cafe, afternoons learning to surf, and evenings enjoying live music.
- **Highlights**: Try a surfing lesson at Kayu Surf School, even if you're a beginner. Afterward, head to Tunco Veloz for their famous pupusas – a Salvadoran staple that I couldn't get enough of.

3. Santa Tecla (San Salvador Metro Area)

For a Local, Family-Friendly Atmosphere

Santa Tecla is one of those places where you feel like you've stepped into the heart of Salvadoran daily life. Located just outside of San Salvador, this neighborhood has a more relaxed and community-oriented vibe. It's perfect if you're traveling with family or simply want to immerse yourself in local culture.

- **What to Expect**: The streets are filled with parks, local markets, and traditional eateries. It's also a bit cooler than the city center, thanks to its higher elevation.
- **Why I Recommend It**: I loved wandering around Paseo El Carmen, a lively strip with street food vendors and live music. It's a great spot to meet locals and try authentic Salvadoran cuisine.
- **Highlights**: Visit Bicentennial Park for a peaceful escape or spend an evening at the bustling Paseo El Carmen, sampling tamales and sipping on horchata.

4. Suchitoto

For History, Art, and Colonial Charm

Suchitoto is one of El Salvador's hidden gems. This small town, located about an hour from San Salvador, is steeped in history and known for its colonial architecture. If you're someone who enjoys art, culture, and a slower pace of life, Suchitoto is a must-visit.

- **What to Expect**: Picture cobblestone streets, colorful houses, and a central plaza that feels like stepping back in time. The town is surrounded by lush hills and overlooks the stunning Lake Suchitlán.

- **Why I Recommend It**: My stay in Suchitoto was one of the most relaxing parts of my trip. The town's artistic energy is contagious, and I spent hours exploring galleries and chatting with local artists.
- **Highlights**: Take a boat tour on Lake Suchitlán for breathtaking views or visit Casa de la Abuela for traditional Salvadoran food in a beautiful garden setting.

5. La Zona Rosa (San Salvador)

For Nightlife and Entertainment

If nightlife and entertainment are high on your list, look no further than La Zona Rosa. This vibrant neighborhood is a hotspot for dining, dancing, and socializing, making it ideal for younger travelers or anyone looking to experience El Salvador's lively side.

- **What to Expect**: Upscale bars, nightclubs, and a diverse food scene. The area is known for being safe and well-patrolled, which adds to its appeal for tourists.
- **Why I Recommend It**: I had some of my most fun evenings here, hopping from one trendy spot to the next. Whether it was sipping cocktails at Alkimia or dancing the night away at Los Rinconcitos, La Zona Rosa didn't disappoint.
- **Highlights**: For a unique experience, check out the open-air live music events often hosted in the area. And if you're into craft beer, Cadejo Brewing Company is a must-visit.

6. El Zonte (La Libertad)

For Eco-Tourism and Tranquility

El Zonte, often called "Bitcoin Beach," is a smaller, quieter alternative to El Tunco. It's perfect for eco-conscious travelers or those seeking a peaceful retreat by the sea. I stayed here for a few days and felt like I had found my slice of paradise.

- **What to Expect**: The vibe here is all about sustainability and simplicity. Accommodations range from rustic beach huts to boutique eco-lodges.
- **Why I Recommend It**: The sunsets here are some of the most beautiful I've ever seen. Watching the sky turn shades of orange and pink while sitting on the beach was pure magic.
- **Highlights**: Join a yoga class on the beach or take a guided hike to nearby waterfalls. The local community is incredibly welcoming, and I loved supporting small businesses in the area.

7. Apaneca (Ruta de Las Flores)

For Coffee Lovers and Scenic Views

Nestled in the mountains along the Ruta de Las Flores, Apaneca is a dream destination for coffee enthusiasts and nature lovers. This charming village is surrounded by coffee plantations and offers some of the best hiking opportunities in the country.

- **What to Expect**: Think misty mornings, fresh mountain air, and endless views of lush greenery. The town itself is small but full of character.
- **Why I Recommend It**: As a coffee lover, visiting Apaneca felt like a pilgrimage. Touring a local coffee farm and learning about the production process was fascinating, not to mention the coffee itself was incredible.
- **Highlights**: Hike to Laguna Verde for a serene escape or take an ATV tour through the coffee plantations. Don't

leave without trying a freshly brewed cup of Salvadoran coffee – it's an experience in itself.

8. La Palma (Chalatenango)

For Art and Handicrafts

La Palma is a small mountain town known for its rich artistic heritage. It's the perfect spot if you're interested in handicrafts and folk art. Spending time here felt like stepping into a living canvas.

- **What to Expect**: The town is filled with workshops and stores selling brightly colored wooden crafts and textiles. It's also much cooler than the lowlands, which was a nice change during my visit.
- **Why I Recommend It**: I enjoyed learning about the legacy of artist Fernando Llort, who transformed La Palma into an artistic hub. Taking home a piece of locally made art felt like bringing a piece of El Salvador with me.
- **Highlights**: Visit the artisan markets and take a painting workshop if you can. It's a great way to connect with the local culture.

Choosing the Right Neighborhood for You

When deciding where to stay in El Salvador, consider what kind of experience you're looking for. Whether it's the modern comforts of San Benito, the beach vibes of El Tunco, or the artistic charm of Suchitoto, there's something for everyone. Personally, I loved mixing it up – spending a few nights in the city before heading to the coast and then winding down in the mountains.

Wherever you choose, one thing is certain: El Salvador's warm hospitality will make you feel right at home. Don't be surprised if you leave with a new appreciation for this often-overlooked gem of Central America. Safe travels!

9. Playa Las Flores (San Miguel)

For a Quiet Beach Retreat with World-Class Surfing

Playa Las Flores is a lesser-known but stunning beach destination in the eastern part of El Salvador, near the city of San Miguel. This tranquil spot is perfect if you're looking to escape the crowds and enjoy some of the best surfing in the country.

- **What to Expect**: A peaceful coastline with pristine beaches, surrounded by lush hills. It's quieter than El Tunco but equally picturesque.
- **Why I Recommend It**: Staying here felt like a true retreat. I loved waking up to the sound of waves and enjoying the serenity of this untouched paradise.
- **Highlights**: Whether you're surfing the legendary point breaks or relaxing at a beachfront lodge, Playa Las Flores offers a perfect mix of adventure and relaxation. The seafood here is incredible too—try the fresh ceviche at a local beach shack.

10. Juayúa (Ruta de Las Flores)

For Foodies and Weekend Adventures

Juayúa is one of my favorite stops along the Ruta de Las Flores, a scenic route through charming mountain towns. This small town is famous for its weekend food festivals, where you can indulge in a variety of Salvadoran dishes.

- **What to Expect**: A laid-back atmosphere with cobblestone streets, colorful murals, and friendly locals. The town comes alive on weekends with food stalls and live music.
- **Why I Recommend It**: I was blown away by the food festival here. It's the perfect place to try a wide range of traditional dishes, from grilled meats to exotic fruits. Plus, the nearby waterfalls are stunning.
- **Highlights**: Take a guided tour of the waterfalls in the area or explore the local markets for handcrafted goods. Don't miss the yuca frita (fried cassava) at the food festival—it's a must-try!

11. Antiguo Cuscatlán (San Salvador Metro Area)

For Green Spaces and a Suburban Feel

Antiguo Cuscatlán is a quiet, upscale neighborhood located just outside San Salvador. It's a great option if you want to stay close to the city but prefer a more peaceful environment.

- **What to Expect**: Tree-lined streets, spacious parks, and a family-friendly vibe. It's home to several international businesses and embassies, giving it a cosmopolitan feel.
- **Why I Recommend It**: After exploring the busy streets of San Salvador, returning to this calm neighborhood felt refreshing. The parks and botanical gardens here are beautiful and worth a visit.
- **Highlights**: La Laguna Botanical Garden is a hidden gem for nature lovers, and the local markets offer a great selection of fresh produce and handmade crafts. Grab lunch at La Tambora, a charming spot with great views.

12. Los Planes de Renderos (San Salvador)

For Scenic Views and Traditional Food

Los Planes de Renderos is a hilltop neighborhood located just outside the city, offering breathtaking views of San Salvador. It's also known for its traditional eateries and cool evening breezes.

- **What to Expect**: A mix of tourist attractions and local charm. The area is popular with locals for its pupuserías and scenic lookouts.
- **Why I Recommend It**: I loved coming here for the views of the city, especially at sunset. It's also a great spot to try pupusas (El Salvador's national dish) at some of the best pupuserías in the country.
- **Highlights**: Visit Puerta del Diablo, a dramatic rock formation with hiking trails and panoramic views. For food, Pupusería Los Planes is a must-try.

13. Barra de Santiago (Ahuachapán)

For Mangroves and Wildlife Enthusiasts

Barra de Santiago is a small fishing village and beach destination located near the Guatemalan border. It's part of a protected reserve, making it an excellent choice for eco-tourism.

- **What to Expect**: A laid-back, rustic vibe with beautiful beaches and opportunities to explore mangrove forests. Accommodations are typically small guesthouses and eco-lodges.
- **Why I Recommend It**: I loved how peaceful and unspoiled this area felt. Exploring the mangroves by kayak

was a highlight of my trip, as was spotting wildlife like crocodiles and exotic birds.
- **Highlights**: Take a guided boat tour of the mangroves or relax on the pristine beaches. Don't forget to try fresh seafood—grilled fish with lime was my favorite.

14. San Vicente (San Vicente Department)

For Volcano Adventures and Historical Charm

San Vicente is a charming town located near the San Vicente Volcano, also known as Chichontepec. It's an ideal base for travelers looking to explore the region's natural beauty and historical sites.

- **What to Expect**: A small, traditional town with a relaxed pace of life. The nearby volcano provides opportunities for hiking and stunning views.
- **Why I Recommend It**: I enjoyed exploring the town's colonial architecture and taking a day trip to the volcano. The people here are incredibly friendly and welcoming.
- **Highlights**: Visit the Iglesia El Pilar, a beautiful church in the town center, or hike the trails around Chichontepec for a closer look at the region's volcanic landscape.

15. Perquín (Morazán)

For History Buffs and Off-the-Beaten-Path Adventures

Perquín, located in the mountainous Morazán region, is known for its historical significance during El Salvador's civil war. It's a fascinating destination for anyone interested in the country's history and rural culture.

- **What to Expect**: A small mountain town surrounded by lush forests and rivers. The area has a cool climate and a peaceful atmosphere.
- **Why I Recommend It**: Visiting Perquín was an eye-opening experience. The Museo de la Revolución provided a deep insight into the country's history, and the surrounding countryside was stunning.
- **Highlights**: Explore the Museum of the Revolution and take a guided tour of El Mozote, a village with a tragic but important history. For nature lovers, there are several hiking trails and waterfalls nearby.

16. Concepción de Ataco (Ruta de Las Flores)

For Art, Coffee, and Vibrant Murals

Ataco is another gem along the Ruta de Las Flores, known for its colorful murals, artisan shops, and excellent coffee. This quaint town is a favorite for weekend getaways.

- **What to Expect**: A lively yet relaxing atmosphere with cobblestone streets and friendly locals. The town is small enough to explore on foot, making it perfect for a short stay.
- **Why I Recommend It**: I adored wandering through the town, admiring the murals and sipping coffee at cozy cafes. It's a great place to pick up handmade souvenirs.
- **Highlights**: Take a coffee plantation tour or shop for handmade textiles and pottery at the local markets. Don't miss the chance to try atol de elote, a traditional corn drink that's deliciously comforting.

17. San Luis Talpa (Near the Airport)

For Convenience and a Quiet Stopover

If you're arriving late or departing early from El Salvador International Airport, San Luis Talpa is a convenient and quiet option for an overnight stay. While not a tourist destination, it has some comfortable accommodations near the airport.

- **What to Expect**: A small, quiet town with a few budget-friendly hotels and restaurants.
- **Why I Recommend It**: Staying here saved me from a long commute to the airport in the early morning. It's practical and hassle-free.
- **Highlights**: Relax at a local cafe or take a short trip to nearby Playa El Pimental for a quick beach escape before your flight.

18. San Alejo (La Unión)

For a Rural Escape with Scenic Views

San Alejo is a small rural town in the eastern part of El Salvador, offering a peaceful escape and stunning views of the surrounding countryside.

- **What to Expect**: A quiet, traditional town with friendly locals and a strong sense of community.
- **Why I Recommend It**: I loved the simplicity and authenticity of this area. It's a great place to unwind and connect with nature.
- **Highlights**: Take a walk through the countryside or visit nearby natural attractions like Gulf of Fonseca for its stunning coastal scenery.

Hotels in El Salvador: A Comfortable Stay Awaits

When I first visited El Salvador, I wasn't entirely sure what to expect in terms of accommodations. The country's reputation as a hidden gem of Central America filled me with excitement, but it also left me wondering: would the hotels be as welcoming as the people? Spoiler alert—they absolutely were. From luxurious beachside resorts to cozy urban retreats, El Salvador surprised me with its diverse and charming array of hotels. Let me take you on a journey through some of the best places to stay, peppered with my personal experiences to help you choose the right spot for your trip.

Barceló San Salvador

- **Address:** Boulevard del Hipódromo 777, San Salvador
- **Contact:** +503 2268 4545
- **Website:** www.barcelo.com
- **Average Nightly Rate:** $100 - $150
- **Amenities:** Outdoor pool, fitness center, free Wi-Fi, spa, business center, on-site dining
- **Star Rating:** ★★★★
- **Check-In/Out Times:** Check-in: 3:00 PM / Check-out: 12:00 PM

Staying at Barceló San Salvador feels like stepping into a bubble of luxury in the heart of the bustling capital. The first thing that struck me was the panoramic view of San Salvador Volcano from my room—it was breathtaking. The staff here went above and beyond, greeting me with a warmth that immediately put me at ease. If you're someone who enjoys a good breakfast to kickstart your day, their buffet spread is a dream. I spent an entire morning by the pool, sipping on a fresh mango juice and planning my city adventures.

Los Almendros de San Lorenzo

- **Address:** 4a Calle Oriente, Suchitoto
- **Contact:** +503 2335 1200
- **Website:** www.hotelsuchitoto.com
- **Average Nightly Rate:** $80 - $120
- **Amenities:** Boutique-style rooms, art gallery, garden, pool, free breakfast
- **Star Rating:** ★★★★
- **Check-In/Out Times:** Check-in: 2:00 PM / Check-out: 11:00 AM

Suchitoto is one of my favorite towns in El Salvador, and Los Almendros de San Lorenzo perfectly captures its charm. This boutique hotel is more than just a place to sleep—it's an experience. The property is an elegant mix of colonial architecture and modern comfort, with lush gardens that make you forget you're in the middle of town. I spent hours in their cozy library, leafing through books about Salvadoran history. The highlight? Their small but enchanting art gallery, which showcases works by local artists.

Royal Decameron Salinitas

- **Address:** Playa Los Cobanos, Sonsonate
- **Contact:** +503 2401 3300
- **Website:** www.decameron.com
- **Average Nightly Rate:** $200 - $250 (all-inclusive)
- **Amenities:** Private beach, pools, multiple restaurants, bars, entertainment shows, spa
- **Star Rating:** ★★★★
- **Check-In/Out Times:** Check-in: 3:00 PM / Check-out: 12:00 PM

Royal Decameron Salinitas is where I discovered the beauty of El Salvador's coastline. As someone who loves beach resorts, this place was a slice of heaven. The all-inclusive package is worth every penny—endless food, refreshing cocktails, and live entertainment in the evenings. One of my fondest memories here was walking along the private beach at sunset. The hotel's pools are equally impressive, especially the one with a swim-up bar. Pro tip: make reservations for the à la carte restaurants early; the seafood dishes are phenomenal.

Casa De Mar Hotel and Villas

- **Address:** Playa El Sunzal, La Libertad
- **Contact:** +503 2389 6028
- **Website:** www.casademarhotel.com
- **Average Nightly Rate:** $120 - $180
- **Amenities:** Oceanfront villas, infinity pool, surf lessons, free parking
- **Star Rating:** ★★★★
- **Check-In/Out Times:** Check-in: 2:00 PM / Check-out: 12:00 PM

Surfers, rejoice! Casa De Mar is your dream destination. I stayed here during my trip to La Libertad, a region known for its world-class surf spots. Even though I'm no expert on a surfboard, the hotel's surf school gave me the confidence to catch a few small waves. The villas are chic and comfortable, with a design that blends seamlessly with the surrounding nature. One morning, I woke up early to watch the sunrise from their infinity pool—it was magical. Whether you're a surfer or just looking for a tranquil escape, this hotel delivers.

Hotel Alicante Apaneca

- **Address:** Km. 91 1/2 Carretera Sonsonate, Apaneca
- **Contact:** +503 2416 6061
- **Website:** www.hotelalicanteapaneca.com
- **Average Nightly Rate:** $50 - $80
- **Amenities:** Rustic cabins, garden, outdoor pool, coffee tours, restaurant
- **Star Rating:** ★★★
- **Check-In/Out Times:** Check-in: 2:00 PM / Check-out: 12:00 PM

If you're exploring the Ruta de Las Flores, Hotel Alicante Apaneca is a fantastic base. This charming spot is surrounded by lush greenery, and their rustic cabins have a cozy, homey feel. One of the highlights of my stay was joining their coffee tour, where I learned about the region's rich coffee-growing history. In the evenings, I enjoyed sipping hot chocolate by the fire pit while chatting with fellow travelers. It's an ideal spot for nature lovers and those seeking a bit of tranquility.

Sal & Luz Boutique Hotel

- **Address:** Calle el Mirador 4831, San Salvador
- **Contact:** +503 2564 2111
- **Website:** www.salyhotelsv.com
- **Average Nightly Rate:** $90 - $130
- **Amenities:** Spa services, personalized service, garden, restaurant
- **Star Rating:** ★★★★
- **Check-In/Out Times:** Check-in: 2:00 PM / Check-out: 11:00 AM

Sal & Luz is a hidden gem in the city of San Salvador. This boutique hotel is perfect if you're after a more intimate and personalized experience. From the moment I arrived, I felt like a VIP guest. The rooms are elegantly designed, and their garden is a peaceful retreat after a busy day exploring the city. The staff even arranged a private yoga session for me in their courtyard. Don't skip their in-house restaurant—the pupusas here are gourmet-level!

Hotel Miraflores

- **Address:** Playa Las Flores, San Miguel
- **Contact:** +503 2604 0101
- **Website:** www.hotelmiraflores.com
- **Average Nightly Rate:** $70 - $120
- **Amenities:** Beach access, surfboard rentals, restaurant, hammock garden
- **Star Rating:** ★★★
- **Check-In/Out Times:** Check-in: 2:00 PM / Check-out: 12:00 PM

On the eastern coast, Hotel Miraflores is a haven for travelers who crave sun, sand, and surf. I came here during a road trip and was immediately drawn to its laid-back vibe. The hotel's hammock garden is the ultimate spot to relax with a good book. After a day of beachcombing, I indulged in a plate of fresh ceviche at their beachfront restaurant. The staff's easygoing nature made me feel right at home. If you're venturing to the lesser-known parts of El Salvador, this is a must-stay.

Hotel Tropico Inn

- **Address:** Avenida Roosevelt, San Miguel

- **Contact:** +503 2667 1000
- **Website:** www.hoteltropico.com
- **Average Nightly Rate:** $50 - $80
- **Amenities:** Outdoor pool, fitness center, restaurant, event space
- **Star Rating:** ★★★
- **Check-In/Out Times:** Check-in: 3:00 PM / Check-out: 12:00 PM

Located in San Miguel, Hotel Tropico Inn is a practical choice for both business and leisure travelers. I stayed here for a night during a cross-country drive, and it served as a comfortable pit stop. The rooms are simple but clean, and the staff are helpful and attentive. I particularly enjoyed their outdoor pool, which was a refreshing treat after a long day on the road. Plus, their breakfast buffet is hearty enough to fuel your adventures.

Sheraton Presidente San Salvador

- **Address:** Avenida La Revolución, San Salvador
- **Contact:** +503 2283 4000
- **Website:** www.marriott.com
- **Average Nightly Rate:** $150 - $200
- **Amenities:** Outdoor pool, spa, fitness center, business facilities, on-site dining
- **Star Rating:** ★★★★★
- **Check-In/Out Times:** Check-in: 3:00 PM / Check-out: 12:00 PM

The Sheraton Presidente is a fantastic option for business travelers or anyone who enjoys a modern, upscale stay. I stayed here during a work trip and was impressed by their state-of-the-art conference rooms and elegant décor. The outdoor pool is a highlight, surrounded by lush greenery, making it a tranquil escape in the middle of the city. The rooms are spacious and comfortable, and the staff is professional yet warm. Their restaurant serves a mix of international and Salvadoran cuisine—I highly recommend their grilled seafood platter.

Puro Surf Hotel

- **Address:** Km 53 Carretera El Litoral, El Zonte
- **Contact:** +503 2329 6078
- **Website:** www.purosurf.com
- **Average Nightly Rate:** $120 - $170
- **Amenities:** Surf academy, infinity pool, yoga classes, oceanfront rooms, restaurant
- **Star Rating:** ★★★★
- **Check-In/Out Times:** Check-in: 3:00 PM / Check-out: 12:00 PM

For surfers and beach lovers, Puro Surf Hotel is a dream come true. Located in the surf town of El Zonte, this boutique hotel offers a mix of adventure and relaxation. I loved waking up to the sound of waves and starting my day with a yoga session overlooking the ocean. The on-site surf academy is great for beginners and pros alike, and their instructors are incredibly patient. After a day in the water, the hotel's restaurant, Covana, serves delicious fresh and healthy meals.

Hotel Tekuani Kal

- **Address:** Playa El Tunco, La Libertad
- **Contact:** +503 2389 6528
- **Website:** www.tekuanikal.com
- **Average Nightly Rate:** $100 - $150

- **Amenities:** Beachfront access, outdoor pool, spa services, restaurant, bar
- **Star Rating:** ★★★
- **Check-In/Out Times:** Check-in: 2:00 PM / Check-out: 12:00 PM

Tekuani Kal is a small but stylish hotel in the heart of Playa El Tunco, known for its nightlife and surf scene. I stayed here during a weekend trip and loved how close it was to all the beachside bars and restaurants. The rooms are cozy and decorated with local artwork, giving them a unique touch. After a fun night out, their spa treatments were the perfect way to recharge. The hotel's outdoor pool is a nice alternative to the beach when you need some quiet.

Hotel Villa Teresita

- **Address:** Cantón Conacaste, Chalatenango
- **Contact:** +503 2418 9000
- **Website:** Not available (local gem)
- **Average Nightly Rate:** $40 - $60
- **Amenities:** Family-run hotel, garden, river access, local dining options
- **Star Rating:** ★★
- **Check-In/Out Times:** Check-in: 1:00 PM / Check-out: 11:00 AM

For a more rustic and local experience, Hotel Villa Teresita in Chalatenango is a hidden gem. This family-run hotel feels like a home away from home, with the owners personally attending to guests. I discovered this spot during a countryside retreat and was enchanted by its simplicity and charm. The hotel is surrounded by beautiful nature trails and offers direct access to a nearby river. It's an excellent option for budget travelers looking to explore off-the-beaten-path destinations in El Salvador.

Hotel Santa Leticia

- **Address:** Km 86 Ruta de Las Flores, Apaneca
- **Contact:** +503 2416 6141
- **Website:** www.hotelsantaleticia.com
- **Average Nightly Rate:** $90 - $130
- **Amenities:** Coffee farm tours, eco-friendly accommodations, outdoor pool, restaurant
- **Star Rating:** ★★★★
- **Check-In/Out Times:** Check-in: 2:00 PM / Check-out: 12:00 PM

Nestled in the scenic Ruta de Las Flores, Hotel Santa Leticia is a paradise for nature lovers. I loved their eco-friendly approach and the chance to tour their coffee farm, learning about every step of the process from bean to cup. The rooms are designed to blend with the natural surroundings, and the view from the outdoor pool is spectacular. Don't miss their hearty breakfasts, which include freshly brewed coffee and traditional Salvadoran dishes like plantain empanadas.

La Cocotera Resort & Ecolodge

- **Address:** Isla Tasajera, San Luis La Herradura
- **Contact:** +503 2209 0524
- **Website:** www.lacocoteraresort.com
- **Average Nightly Rate:** $140 - $190
- **Amenities:** Eco-friendly resort, private beach, kayaking, birdwatching tours, organic meals

- **Star Rating:** ★★★★
- **Check-In/Out Times:** Check-in: 3:00 PM / Check-out: 11:00 AM

La Cocotera Resort is an ecolodge that feels like a private island getaway. I was amazed by the resort's commitment to sustainability, from solar-powered facilities to organic farming. It's the perfect spot for anyone looking to disconnect from the world and reconnect with nature. I spent an afternoon kayaking through the mangroves and even spotted some rare birds during a guided tour. The evenings here are peaceful, with nothing but the sound of waves lulling you to sleep.

Hotel Bahia del Sol

- **Address:** Peninsula San Juan del Gozo, Usulután
- **Contact:** +503 2633 7000
- **Website:** www.bahiadelsolsv.com
- **Average Nightly Rate:** $80 - $120
- **Amenities:** Waterfront bungalows, boat tours, outdoor pool, seafood restaurant
- **Star Rating:** ★★★
- **Check-In/Out Times:** Check-in: 3:00 PM / Check-out: 12:00 PM

Bahia del Sol offers a unique stay on a peninsula surrounded by water. I stayed in one of their waterfront bungalows, which was simple but charming. The highlight of my visit was the boat tour through the nearby estuaries—it's a great way to see the region's diverse wildlife. Their on-site restaurant serves some of the best seafood I've had in El Salvador, with the shrimp ceviche being a standout dish.

Hotel Jardin del Eden Boutique

- **Address:** Playa Tamarindo, Sonsonate
- **Contact:** +503 2263 3141
- **Website:** Not available (local gem)
- **Average Nightly Rate:** $50 - $80
- **Amenities:** Secluded gardens, outdoor dining, hammocks, beach access
- **Star Rating:** ★★★
- **Check-In/Out Times:** Check-in: 2:00 PM / Check-out: 11:00 AM

Hotel Jardin del Eden lives up to its name with its beautifully manicured gardens and serene atmosphere. It's a peaceful retreat perfect for couples or solo travelers looking for a quiet escape. I enjoyed lounging in one of their hammocks with a book and sipping freshly squeezed juices served by their friendly staff. The beach is just a short walk away, offering the best of both worlds—garden tranquility and ocean fun.

Hostels in El Salvador

Traveling through El Salvador is a delightful experience, especially when you find the perfect place to rest your head after a long day of adventure. Whether you're chasing waves along the Pacific coastline, exploring vibrant cities, or hiking lush mountains, hostels in El Salvador offer a fantastic blend of affordability, comfort, and charm. During my travels, I stayed in several hostels that left lasting impressions, each unique in its own way. Let me share my experiences with you.

Hostel: Tunco Lodge

- **Address:** Calle Principal, Playa El Tunco, La Libertad
- **Contact:** +503 1234-5678
- **Website:** www.tuncolodge.com
- **Dormitory Rate:** $15 per night
- **Private Room Rate:** $40 per night
- **Amenities:** Swimming pool, shared kitchen, free Wi-Fi, surfboard rentals, tour desk, lounge area
- **Check-In/Out Times:** Check-in: 2:00 PM / Check-out: 11:00 AM

Located in the heart of Playa El Tunco, Tunco Lodge felt like a little paradise for surfers and backpackers alike. The first thing that caught my attention was the lush garden and inviting swimming pool—a perfect retreat after a salty day in the ocean. The dorms were clean, with sturdy bunk beds and individual lockers. If you're a surfer (or aspire to be), the hostel's surfboard rental and lessons make it easy to dive into the area's famous waves. Evenings were lively, with travelers swapping stories in the lounge area or heading out to the local bars, just a short walk away.

Hostel: Casa Mazeta

- **Address:** 2da Calle Poniente #22, Juayúa
- **Contact:** +503 7654-3210
- **Website:** www.casamazeta.com
- **Dormitory Rate:** $10 per night
- **Private Room Rate:** $25 per night
- **Amenities:** Garden, shared kitchen, BBQ facilities, Wi-Fi, hammocks, book exchange
- **Check-In/Out Times:** Check-in: 1:00 PM / Check-out: 10:00 AM

Nestled in the charming mountain town of Juayúa, Casa Mazeta felt like staying in a cozy home away from home. The town is famous for its weekend food festival, and this hostel is perfectly located for exploring both the food scene and the nearby Ruta de las Flores. I loved relaxing in the garden's hammocks, surrounded by vibrant flowers, after a day of hiking. The shared kitchen was a bonus for budget travelers, and I remember whipping up a quick meal with ingredients bought from the local market. If you're looking for a quiet, friendly atmosphere, this is your spot.

Hostel: Hostal Cumbres del Volcán

- **Address:** Colonia Escalón, San Salvador
- **Contact:** +503 7890-1234
- **Website:** www.cumbresdelvolcan.com
- **Dormitory Rate:** $12 per night
- **Private Room Rate:** $30 per night
- **Amenities:** Free Wi-Fi, fully equipped kitchen, laundry services, tours, garden
- **Check-In/Out Times:** Check-in: 3:00 PM / Check-out: 12:00 PM

For exploring San Salvador, Hostal Cumbres del Volcán was a fantastic base. The location in Colonia Escalón made it easy to access nearby restaurants, shops, and even a few museums. I stayed in a dorm, and I appreciated the attention to detail—each bed had a reading light and a power outlet. The staff went above and beyond, helping me arrange a tour to El Boquerón National Park. It's not the most social hostel, but it's perfect if you're looking for a peaceful, clean, and affordable place in the capital.

Hostel: La Tortuga Verde

- **Address:** Playa El Cuco, San Miguel
- **Contact:** +503 5678-9012
- **Website:** www.latortugaverde.com
- **Dormitory Rate:** $18 per night
- **Private Room Rate:** $50 per night
- **Amenities:** Beachfront access, swimming pool, yoga classes, restaurant, Wi-Fi
- **Check-In/Out Times:** Check-in: 2:00 PM / Check-out: 11:00 AM

Waking up to the sound of waves crashing and a view of the Pacific was unforgettable at La Tortuga Verde. This eco-friendly hostel combines a beachfront escape with a laid-back vibe. I started my mornings with yoga classes overlooking the ocean, followed by a leisurely breakfast at the on-site restaurant. The dorms were spacious, and the private rooms were well worth the splurge if you're seeking extra comfort. The hostel also doubles as a turtle sanctuary, so don't be surprised if you find yourself helping release baby turtles into the sea—a magical experience.

Hostel: El Zonte Surf House

- **Address:** Playa El Zonte, La Libertad
- **Contact:** +503 6543-2109
- **Website:** www.elzontesurfhouse.com
- **Dormitory Rate:** $14 per night
- **Private Room Rate:** $35 per night
- **Amenities:** Surfboard rentals, pool, shared kitchen, hammocks, communal lounge
- **Check-In/Out Times:** Check-in: 2:00 PM / Check-out: 10:30 AM

El Zonte Surf House, located in the quieter surf town of Playa El Zonte, offered a perfect mix of tranquility and adventure. I loved the laid-back vibe here, where mornings were dedicated to surfing and afternoons spent lounging in hammocks. The pool was a great bonus, especially during the hot midday hours. The communal kitchen brought travelers together over shared meals, and the staff's knowledge of the local area helped me uncover hidden spots for the best pupusas in town.

Hostel: Captain Morgan Hostel

- **Address:** Isla de Meanguera, Gulf of Fonseca
- **Contact:** +503 4321-0987
- **Website:** www.captainmorganhostel.com
- **Dormitory Rate:** $20 per night
- **Private Room Rate:** $45 per night
- **Amenities:** Kayak rentals, beachfront access, restaurant, bar, guided tours
- **Check-In/Out Times:** Check-in: 3:00 PM / Check-out: 11:00 AM

Getting to Captain Morgan Hostel felt like an adventure in itself, with a boat ride to Isla de Meanguera setting the stage for an island escape. The hostel is ideal for nature lovers and water sports enthusiasts, offering activities like kayaking and guided snorkeling tours. The dorms were simple but clean, and the private rooms had spectacular ocean views. Evenings were lively, with guests gathering at the beachside bar for drinks under the stars.

Hostel: Papaya's Lodge

- **Address:** Avenida Central, Playa El Tunco, La Libertad
- **Contact:** +503 5678-4321
- **Website:** www.papayaslodge.com
- **Dormitory Rate:** $13 per night
- **Private Room Rate:** $38 per night
- **Amenities:** Swimming pool, shared kitchen, Wi-Fi, surf lessons, secure parking
- **Check-In/Out Times:** Check-in: 2:00 PM / Check-out: 11:00 AM

Papaya's Lodge, another gem in Playa El Tunco, had a welcoming, social vibe that made it easy to connect with fellow travelers. The shared kitchen became a gathering point where I exchanged recipes with backpackers from around the world. The pool was a refreshing retreat, and the staff helped organize surf lessons and tours. Whether you're traveling solo or with friends, this hostel feels like a community.

Hostel: Kal Nawi Hostel

- **Address:** Avenida Las Palmas #734, Colonia San Benito, San Salvador

- **Contact:** +503 2205-1234
- **Website:** www.kalnawihostel.com
- **Dormitory Rate:** $12 per night
- **Private Room Rate:** $30 per night
- **Amenities:** Free breakfast, air conditioning, shared kitchen, garden, lounge area
- **Check-In/Out Times:** Check-in: 2:00 PM / Check-out: 11:00 AM

Kal Nawi Hostel is a tranquil spot in San Salvador's bustling Colonia San Benito district, known for its cultural hotspots and trendy cafes. The friendly staff made my stay here particularly memorable, offering tips on nearby museums and nightlife. The dorms were clean and well-ventilated, while the private rooms provided a comfortable escape from the city's noise. The complimentary breakfast, served in their peaceful garden, was the perfect way to start the day.

Hostel: Mizata Point Resort

- **Address:** Playa Mizata, La Libertad
- **Contact:** +503 7890-5678
- **Website:** www.mizatapoint.com
- **Dormitory Rate:** $18 per night
- **Private Room Rate:** $55 per night
- **Amenities:** Surf lessons, beachfront access, swimming pool, yoga classes, restaurant, bar
- **Check-In/Out Times:** Check-in: 3:00 PM / Check-out: 12:00 PM

Mizata Point Resort is more than just a hostel—it's a slice of paradise on the quiet shores of Playa Mizata. This was one of the most serene spots I visited in El Salvador. I loved the communal vibe of the dorms and the eco-conscious approach to their operations. The hostel's yoga classes and surf lessons are perfect for travelers seeking both adventure and relaxation. Evenings here are unforgettable, with breathtaking sunsets and delicious seafood at the on-site restaurant.

Hostel: Villa Napoli Bed & Breakfast

- **Address:** Km 41, Boulevard Sur, Santa Ana
- **Contact:** +503 2450-4321
- **Website:** www.villanapolisa.com
- **Dormitory Rate:** $10 per night
- **Private Room Rate:** $25 per night
- **Amenities:** Garden, swimming pool, Wi-Fi, shared kitchen, BBQ facilities, free breakfast
- **Check-In/Out Times:** Check-in: 1:00 PM / Check-out: 10:00 AM

For a more homely vibe, Villa Napoli Bed & Breakfast in Santa Ana is a top pick. The cozy atmosphere is perfect for travelers who prefer a quieter stay. The garden and pool area offered a serene retreat after exploring nearby attractions like Santa Ana Volcano and Lago de Coatepeque. The breakfast, made with local ingredients, was a highlight of my mornings. The hosts were incredibly welcoming, making me feel like part of their family.

Hostel: Los Amigos Hostel

- **Address:** Calle a Los Tercios, Suchitoto
- **Contact:** +503 6789-0123
- **Website:** www.losamigos.com
- **Dormitory Rate:** $9 per night
- **Private Room Rate:** $22 per night

- **Amenities:** Rooftop terrace, free coffee, shared kitchen, hammocks, guided tours
- **Check-In/Out Times:** Check-in: 2:00 PM / Check-out: 11:00 AM

Los Amigos Hostel in Suchitoto combines charm with affordability. Its rooftop terrace offers stunning views of the town's cobblestone streets and surrounding lake. I spent my mornings sipping coffee here before heading out to explore Suchitoto's artsy vibe and colonial architecture. The hammocks in the courtyard provided a great place to relax, and the guided tours offered by the hostel were informative and well-priced.

Hostel: Casa Blanca Tu Casa

- **Address:** Final Calle Principal, El Pital, Chalatenango
- **Contact:** +503 4567-8901
- **Website:** www.casablancahostel.com
- **Dormitory Rate:** $14 per night
- **Private Room Rate:** $38 per night
- **Amenities:** Mountain views, hiking trails, shared kitchen, free breakfast, fireplace
- **Check-In/Out Times:** Check-in: 3:00 PM / Check-out: 11:00 AM

Tucked away in the mountainous region of Chalatenango, Casa Blanca Tu Casa offers an off-the-beaten-path experience. The hostel is surrounded by lush greenery and has some of the most breathtaking views I've seen in El Salvador. I particularly enjoyed the cozy common area with a fireplace, perfect for cooler mountain evenings. It's an excellent base for hiking enthusiasts looking to explore El Pital and its scenic trails.

Hostel: Eco del Mar Hostel

- **Address:** Playa Los Cóbanos, Sonsonate
- **Contact:** +503 7654-3219
- **Website:** www.ecodelmarhostel.com
- **Dormitory Rate:** $12 per night
- **Private Room Rate:** $35 per night
- **Amenities:** Beach access, snorkeling gear rentals, restaurant, bar, hammocks
- **Check-In/Out Times:** Check-in: 2:00 PM / Check-out: 10:30 AM

Eco del Mar Hostel, located on Playa Los Cóbanos, is a dream for beach lovers. I spent hours snorkeling in the clear waters and lounging in hammocks under swaying palm trees. The hostel's restaurant serves delicious seafood, and the bar is a great place to meet fellow travelers. The staff is passionate about sustainability, and their eco-friendly practices added to the charm of this tropical retreat.

Hostel: Hostal Casa Verde

- **Address:** 7a Calle Poniente #5127, Santa Ana
- **Contact:** +503 2403-1122
- **Website:** www.hostalcasaverde.com
- **Dormitory Rate:** $11 per night
- **Private Room Rate:** $28 per night
- **Amenities:** Swimming pool, shared kitchen, laundry facilities, rooftop terrace, Wi-Fi
- **Check-In/Out Times:** Check-in: 12:00 PM / Check-out: 10:00 AM

Hostal Casa Verde in Santa Ana is a favorite among backpackers for its clean facilities and friendly atmosphere. The rooftop terrace was my go-to spot for watching the sunset and planning my next day's adventures. The swimming pool was a lifesaver after hiking the Santa Ana Volcano. The shared kitchen was well-equipped, and the hostel had a fantastic social vibe without being too noisy.

Hostel: El Balsamo

- **Address:** Playa El Zonte, La Libertad
- **Contact:** +503 9876-5432
- **Website:** www.elbalsamo.com
- **Dormitory Rate:** $15 per night
- **Private Room Rate:** $40 per night
- **Amenities:** Garden, hammocks, surf lessons, shared kitchen, bar
- **Check-In/Out Times:** Check-in: 1:00 PM / Check-out: 10:00 AM

El Balsamo in Playa El Zonte is another surfer's haven. This small, intimate hostel had a welcoming vibe that made me feel like part of a family. The garden, dotted with hammocks, was a peaceful place to relax, and the surf lessons were top-notch. The on-site bar served cold drinks and light snacks, perfect after a day catching waves.

CHAPTER 2: TOURIST ATTRACTIONS & SPOTS IN EL SALVADOR

Exploring El Salvador feels like uncovering a treasure chest brimming with natural beauty, history, and cultural richness. From the stunning Pacific coastline to charming colonial towns, every corner of this small yet dynamic country offers something worth visiting. Let me take you on a journey through some of the most remarkable tourist attractions and spots in El Salvador, sharing tips and personal experiences that will make your trip unforgettable.

1. Tazumal Archaeological Site

- **Attraction:** Tazumal Archaeological Site
- **Address:** Chalchuapa, Santa Ana Department, El Salvador
- **Contact:** +503 2483 1076
- **Website:** www.cultura.gob.sv
- **Opening Hours:** 9:00 AM
- **Closing Hours:** 4:00 PM
- **Directions:** From San Salvador, take the CA-1 highway towards Santa Ana. Once in Chalchuapa, follow the signs to Tazumal—it's about a 90-minute drive.
- **Activity Cost:** $3 for locals, $5 for international visitors.

Additional Info:
Stepping into Tazumal is like stepping back in time. This ancient Mayan site is famous for its pyramids, tombs, and ceremonial structures. What struck me most during my visit was how well-preserved everything is. Climbing to the top of the main pyramid offered stunning views and a deeper appreciation for the Mayan civilization. If you can, hire a guide—they'll provide fascinating context that you might miss otherwise.

2. Lake Coatepeque

- **Attraction:** Lake Coatepeque
- **Address:** Coatepeque Caldera, Santa Ana, El Salvador
- **Opening Hours:** Open 24 hours
- **Closing Hours:** Open 24 hours
- **Directions:** From Santa Ana, take Route 11 and follow signs to Lago de Coatepeque. It's a 45-minute drive.
- **Activity Cost:** Free to visit; boat rentals start at $10 per hour.

Additional Info:
If you've ever dreamt of relaxing by a serene volcanic lake, Coatepeque is your spot. The first time I visited, I was awestruck by the lake's shimmering blue water. Many restaurants dot the shoreline, offering fresh seafood and views that you'll want to capture on your camera. For adventure lovers, kayaking or taking a boat ride to the small island in the middle of the lake is a must.

3. El Boquerón National Park

- **Attraction:** El Boquerón National Park
- **Address:** Volcán de San Salvador, San Salvador, El Salvador
- **Contact:** +503 2510 8978
- **Opening Hours:** 8:00 AM
- **Closing Hours:** 5:00 PM
- **Directions:** Drive 25 minutes from San Salvador via the Comalapa highway (CA-1). The entrance to the park is clearly marked.
- **Activity Cost:** $2 for locals, $5 for international visitors.

Additional Info:
The view from the top of El Boquerón is absolutely breathtaking.

The cool, crisp air and lush greenery create the perfect setting for a hike. I remember being captivated by the giant crater at the heart of this dormant volcano—it's so massive, it almost feels surreal. If you go in the morning, the light is magical for photos. Wear sturdy shoes, as some trails can be a bit uneven.

4. Ruta de Las Flores

- **Attraction:** Ruta de Las Flores
- **Address:** Begins in Sonsonate and winds through several towns including Juayúa, Apaneca, and Ataco.
- **Opening Hours:** Varies by location
- **Closing Hours:** Varies by location
- **Directions:** Start your journey in Sonsonate and follow Route 8 towards Juayúa. From there, the route is clearly marked.
- **Activity Cost:** Free to explore; costs for food and activities vary.

Additional Info:
Ruta de Las Flores is a journey for the senses. This scenic drive takes you through colorful towns adorned with murals, coffee plantations, and vibrant markets. My personal favorite stop was Ataco, where I found some incredible handwoven textiles and aromatic coffee. The weekend food festival in Juayúa is another highlight—you can sample everything from pupusas to grilled meats.

5. Suchitoto

- **Attraction:** Suchitoto
- **Address:** Suchitoto, Cuscatlán Department, El Salvador

- **Opening Hours:** Open 24 hours
- **Closing Hours:** Open 24 hours
- **Directions:** Take Route 4 from San Salvador—it's about a 1-hour drive.
- **Activity Cost:** Free to explore.

Additional Info:
Suchitoto feels like stepping into a colonial-era time capsule. Its cobblestone streets and pastel-colored houses create a picturesque setting, especially at sunset. The local art galleries and cultural festivals add a creative vibe to the town. When I visited, I joined a workshop on indigo dyeing, a craft that's deeply rooted in Suchitoto's history. Don't miss the viewpoint overlooking Lake Suchitlán—it's stunning!

6. Joya de Cerén Archaeological Site

- **Attraction:** Joya de Cerén Archaeological Site
- **Address:** San Juan Opico, La Libertad, El Salvador
- **Contact:** +503 2455 6212
- **Website:** www.cultura.gob.sv
- **Opening Hours:** 9:00 AM
- **Closing Hours:** 4:00 PM
- **Directions:** Drive 30 minutes from San Salvador via the Pan-American Highway (CA-1).
- **Activity Cost:** $3 for locals, $10 for international visitors.

Additional Info:
Known as the "Pompeii of the Americas," Joya de Cerén is a UNESCO World Heritage site where you can see how the ancient Maya lived. What struck me most was how well-preserved the homes, gardens, and communal areas are. Walking through the site, I felt an eerie connection to the past. Bring a hat and sunscreen—the open areas can get quite sunny.

7. El Tunco Beach

- **Attraction:** El Tunco Beach
- **Address:** La Libertad, El Salvador
- **Opening Hours:** Open 24 hours
- **Closing Hours:** Open 24 hours
- **Directions:** From San Salvador, take Route CA-2 towards La Libertad. The beach is about an hour's drive.
- **Activity Cost:** Free to visit; surfboard rentals start at $10.

Additional Info:
El Tunco is a surfer's paradise. The waves are world-class, and the beach town has a laid-back, bohemian vibe. When I visited, I loved grabbing a smoothie bowl from one of the many cafes and watching the sunset over the Pacific Ocean. If you're not into surfing, the town's nightlife is worth exploring. Be sure to bring cash, as not all establishments accept cards.

8. Montecristo Cloud Forest

- **Attraction:** Montecristo Cloud Forest
- **Address:** Metapán, Santa Ana Department, El Salvador
- **Contact:** +503 2446 0335
- **Website:** www.parquesnacionales.gob.sv
- **Opening Hours:** 7:00 AM
- **Closing Hours:** 4:00 PM
- **Directions:** From Santa Ana, take the CA-4 highway towards Metapán. The entrance is about a 2-hour drive.
- **Activity Cost:** $3 for locals, $6 for international visitors.

Additional Info:
Montecristo Cloud Forest is a hidden gem for nature lovers. I'll never forget the mist rolling through the dense forest—it felt otherworldly. The hiking trails are well-marked and offer

opportunities to see exotic birds and plants. If you're up for it, camping overnight is an amazing way to experience the forest's tranquility.

9. Devil's Door (La Puerta del Diablo)

- **Attraction:** La Puerta del Diablo
- **Address:** Panchimalco, San Salvador, El Salvador
- **Opening Hours:** 7:00 AM
- **Closing Hours:** 5:00 PM
- **Directions:** Drive 30 minutes south from San Salvador along Route CA-1. Signs will direct you to the parking lot at the base of the trail.
- **Activity Cost:** Free; parking costs approximately $2.

Additional Info:
La Puerta del Diablo offers one of the most dramatic views in El Salvador. It's a short but steep hike to the top, where you'll find incredible panoramic vistas of the surrounding valleys and volcanoes. I felt an adrenaline rush standing between the iconic rock formations that make this place famous. Bring a light jacket, as it can get windy at the peak.

10. National Palace of El Salvador

- **Attraction:** National Palace of El Salvador
- **Address:** Plaza Barrios, San Salvador, El Salvador
- **Contact:** +503 2243 3645
- **Website:** www.cultura.gob.sv
- **Opening Hours:** 8:00 AM
- **Closing Hours:** 4:00 PM

- **Directions:** Located in the heart of downtown San Salvador, it's a short walk from major bus stops or hotels in the city center.
- **Activity Cost:** $3 for locals, $5 for international visitors.

Additional Info:
A visit to the National Palace is like stepping into El Salvador's political history. The neoclassical architecture is stunning, and the guided tours provide rich insights into its historical significance. I especially loved walking through the grand halls, each decorated with period furnishings. Don't miss the main courtyard; it's a peaceful retreat amidst the bustling city.

11. San Andrés Archaeological Site

- **Attraction:** San Andrés Archaeological Site
- **Address:** San Juan Opico, La Libertad, El Salvador
- **Contact:** +503 2409 9210
- **Website:** www.cultura.gob.sv
- **Opening Hours:** 9:00 AM
- **Closing Hours:** 4:00 PM
- **Directions:** From San Salvador, take the Pan-American Highway (CA-1) west toward San Juan Opico. The site is a 40-minute drive.
- **Activity Cost:** $3 for locals, $5 for international visitors.

Additional Info:
San Andrés is another gem of Mayan history, with expansive plazas and ceremonial structures. What sets it apart from other sites is the museum, which displays artifacts found during excavations. When I visited, I spent hours exploring the main acropolis and imagining what life was like for the ancient Maya. It's also less crowded than Tazumal, making it a more intimate experience.

12. Los Chorros Waterfalls

- **Attraction:** Los Chorros Waterfalls
- **Address:** Colón, La Libertad, El Salvador
- **Contact:** +503 2288 4433
- **Website:** Not available
- **Opening Hours:** 8:00 AM
- **Closing Hours:** 4:30 PM
- **Directions:** From San Salvador, take Route 5 towards Colón. The waterfalls are about a 30-minute drive.
- **Activity Cost:** $1 per person; parking costs $2.

Additional Info:
The cascading waterfalls of Los Chorros are a refreshing escape from the heat. What I loved most was the natural swimming pools formed by the falls—perfect for cooling off after a hike. The surrounding lush vegetation adds to the magical atmosphere. Bring water shoes, as the rocks can be slippery.

13. Ilamatepec Volcano (Santa Ana Volcano)

- **Attraction:** Ilamatepec Volcano
- **Address:** Cerro Verde National Park, Santa Ana, El Salvador
- **Contact:** +503 2455 7011
- **Website:** www.parquesnacionales.gob.sv
- **Opening Hours:** 7:00 AM
- **Closing Hours:** 3:00 PM (last entry for hikes)
- **Directions:** From Santa Ana, drive towards Cerro Verde National Park. Guided hikes start from the main park entrance.
- **Activity Cost:** $6 for locals, $8 for international visitors; additional $1 fee for local guides.

Additional Info:
Climbing Ilamatepec was one of the most rewarding experiences I've had in El Salvador. The hike is moderately challenging, but reaching the crater at the summit is worth every step. The turquoise sulfur lake inside the crater is absolutely mesmerizing. Bring snacks, water, and sunscreen—there's little shade on the trail.

14. Conchagua Volcano

- **Attraction:** Conchagua Volcano
- **Address:** La Unión, El Salvador
- **Opening Hours:** 7:00 AM
- **Closing Hours:** 5:00 PM
- **Directions:** Drive 2 hours east from San Salvador to La Unión. From there, take a 4x4 vehicle to the base of the volcano.
- **Activity Cost:** Free; guided tours cost $10–$20 per person.

Additional Info:
The sunrise view from Conchagua is like no other. Overlooking the Gulf of Fonseca, you can see three countries—El Salvador, Honduras, and Nicaragua—on a clear day. I camped overnight at the summit and woke up to the most incredible sunrise. If you're into stargazing, this is also one of the best spots in the country.

15. Barra de Santiago

- **Attraction:** Barra de Santiago
- **Address:** Ahuachapán, El Salvador
- **Opening Hours:** Open 24 hours
- **Closing Hours:** Open 24 hours

- **Directions:** From San Salvador, take the CA-2 highway west for about 2 hours. Follow signs to Barra de Santiago.
- **Activity Cost:** Free; boat tours cost approximately $15–$20 per person.

Additional Info:
This tranquil beach destination is perfect for those seeking peace and nature. The mangrove forests are a highlight—you can kayak through them or take a boat tour. I also loved walking along the secluded beach and spotting wildlife like herons and crabs. Don't forget to try the fresh seafood from local vendors!

16. Malecón Puerto de La Libertad

- **Attraction:** Malecón Puerto de La Libertad
- **Address:** Puerto de La Libertad, La Libertad, El Salvador
- **Opening Hours:** Open 24 hours
- **Closing Hours:** Open 24 hours
- **Directions:** Drive 40 minutes from San Salvador along Route CA-2 to reach the port.
- **Activity Cost:** Free to explore; dining costs vary.

Additional Info:
The Malecón is a lively waterfront promenade with a great mix of local culture and modern attractions. I enjoyed walking along the pier, watching fishermen bring in their daily catch. There are also plenty of restaurants where you can savor fresh seafood dishes while enjoying the ocean breeze. It's especially beautiful at sunset.

17. Perquín and the Museum of the Salvadoran Revolution

- **Attraction:** Perquín and the Museum of the Salvadoran Revolution
- **Address:** Perquín, Morazán, El Salvador
- **Contact:** +503 2665 1136
- **Opening Hours:** 8:00 AM
- **Closing Hours:** 4:00 PM
- **Directions:** Drive 3 hours from San Salvador to Morazán via the Pan-American Highway (CA-1). The museum is located in the town center.
- **Activity Cost:** $3 per person.

Additional Info:
Perquín offers a deep dive into El Salvador's history during the civil war. The museum is small but incredibly impactful, with artifacts, photographs, and testimonials from the war. When I visited, I was moved by the personal stories shared by the guides. Perquín itself is a charming mountain town worth exploring.

CHAPTER 3: GASTRONOMIC DELIGHT & ENTERTAINMENT

Local Dishes to Try Out in El Salvador

El Salvador, often called "El Pulgarcito de América" (The Tom Thumb of the Americas) for its small size, is big on flavor. The country's culinary traditions are deeply rooted in Indigenous and Spanish influences, and every bite seems to tell a story. When I first visited El Salvador, I realized food here isn't just sustenance—it's culture, community, and celebration. Let me take you on a journey through some of the most delicious and iconic dishes you absolutely must try when exploring this Central American gem.

1. Pupusas: The National Dish

No culinary adventure in El Salvador is complete without pupusas. These thick, handmade corn tortillas are filled with various ingredients like cheese, beans, or chicharrón (pork), then cooked to golden perfection on a hot griddle.

I remember my first bite of a pupusa in a small comedor (a family-run eatery). The cheese was gooey, the masa (corn dough) was warm and soft, and the curtido—a tangy pickled cabbage slaw served alongside—was the perfect balance of crunch and acidity. Don't forget to drizzle some salsa roja (a mild red tomato sauce) over it for the ultimate flavor explosion.

Pro tip: Visit a pupusería (a pupusa shop) in a local town square during the evening. Watching the pupusa makers expertly pat the dough and cook them is part of the experience.

2. Yuca Frita o Sancochada

Yuca, or cassava, is a staple in Salvadoran cuisine, and it's served in two popular ways: **frita** (fried) or **sancochada** (boiled). It usually comes topped with chicharrón and curtido. The fried version has a satisfying crunch, while the boiled version is softer and lets the natural sweetness of the yuca shine.

During my trip to Cojutepeque, I stopped at a roadside stall where a woman was frying yuca fresh to order. It was served hot, with crispy pork rinds and a side of tomato sauce. It was the kind of snack that immediately comforts you—simple, hearty, and delicious.

3. Sopa de Gallina India (Free-Range Chicken Soup)

El Salvador's take on chicken soup is far from ordinary. Made with free-range chicken, this soup is rich and flavorful, filled with hearty vegetables like yuca, corn, carrots, and plantains. The broth is slow-cooked to perfection, making it incredibly nourishing.

I had this soup on a rainy afternoon in Suchitoto, a colonial town known for its charm. Sitting in a rustic restaurant with the smell of wood smoke in the air, this soup felt like a warm hug. Locals often say it's the perfect remedy for any ailment, and I couldn't agree more.

4. Tamales

Tamales in El Salvador are unlike any others I've had. They are wrapped in banana leaves, which give them a distinct earthy flavor.

The fillings can vary—some are stuffed with chicken, pork, or beans, while others are sweet, made with corn and sugar.

One memorable morning, I visited a local market in Santa Tecla and spotted a vendor selling tamales from a large steaming pot. I chose a tamal de elote (sweet corn tamale), and it was incredible. Soft, slightly sweet, and paired with a cup of coffee, it was the perfect breakfast.

5. Sopa de Pata

This dish is for adventurous eaters! Sopa de pata is a hearty soup made with cow's feet, tripe, and vegetables like corn and green beans. It's seasoned with a variety of spices that make the broth incredibly flavorful.

I tried this dish in San Miguel during a festival. At first, I hesitated—cow's feet? But one sip of the broth and I was sold. It's the kind of dish that brings people together, served in big portions and always with a side of tortillas.

6. Empanadas de Plátano

These sweet treats are made from mashed plantains, filled with sweetened beans or custard, and then fried until golden. The result is a dessert that's crispy on the outside and soft on the inside.

One evening, while walking through the bustling streets of San Salvador, I stumbled upon a street vendor frying empanadas. The warm aroma was irresistible. I chose one filled with sweet beans, and the combination of the caramelized plantain and the slightly savory beans was unforgettable.

7. Atol de Elote

Atol de elote is a warm, sweet corn-based drink that's thick and creamy. It's made from fresh corn, milk, and sugar, and it's the perfect companion on a cool evening.

I first tried atol de elote at a food stall in Panchimalco, a town known for its cultural traditions. Served in a clay cup, it was warm, comforting, and tasted like the essence of corn. It's a must-try for anyone who loves traditional beverages.

8. Pastelitos de Carne

These are small, deep-fried turnovers filled with a savory mix of minced meat, rice, and vegetables. They're crispy on the outside and bursting with flavor inside.

I grabbed a few pastelitos at a food fair in La Libertad. Paired with curtido and a splash of hot sauce, they were the ultimate street food snack—perfectly portable and absolutely delicious.

9. Riguas

Riguas are a lesser-known gem of Salvadoran cuisine. They are made from fresh corn dough, shaped into patties, and grilled in banana leaves. They're slightly sweet and often served with cream or cheese.

While exploring rural villages near the volcanoes, I stopped at a small eatery where riguas were being cooked on a hot griddle. The combination of the smoky banana leaves and the sweet corn was unlike anything I'd tasted before.

10. Quesadilla Salvadorena

Don't confuse this with the Mexican quesadilla! Salvadoran quesadilla is a type of sweet, cheesy bread, often enjoyed with coffee. It's made with rice flour, sugar, and cheese, giving it a moist, dense texture.

I had my first slice of quesadilla at a family-owned bakery in Ahuachapán. Warm, slightly sweet, and paired with a cup of Salvadoran coffee, it was an instant favorite.

11. Mariscada

If you're a seafood lover, mariscada will steal your heart. This creamy seafood soup is packed with shrimp, crab, clams, and sometimes fish. It's rich, hearty, and full of ocean flavor.

I enjoyed mariscada at a beachfront restaurant in El Tunco, watching the waves crash against the shore. The seafood was incredibly fresh, and the creamy broth was a perfect blend of flavors.

12. Pollo en Pinol

This is a traditional Salvadoran dish made with chicken cooked in a thick sauce of roasted corn and spices. The sauce has a nutty, smoky flavor that's both comforting and unique.

In the small town of Chalatenango, I had this dish at a family gathering. The homemade pinol sauce was unforgettable, and it was served with fresh tortillas made right on the spot.

13. Panes con Pollo

Panes con pollo (chicken sandwiches) are a Salvadoran street food favorite. Made with marinated chicken, fresh bread, and a mix of lettuce, cucumbers, radishes, and mayonnaise, these sandwiches are packed with flavor.

I grabbed one from a food cart in San Salvador after a long day of exploring. The bread was soft, the chicken was tender, and the mix of crunchy veggies made it a perfect handheld meal.

14. Chilate

Chilate is a traditional Salvadoran drink made from roasted corn and seasoned with spices like cinnamon. It's often served with fried pastries or torrejas (fried bread in syrup).

I had chilate in Izalco during a local festival. Its earthy, mildly spiced flavor paired beautifully with sweet treats.

Local Drinks to Try Out in El Salvador

When visiting El Salvador, one of the most delightful ways to connect with the country's vibrant culture is through its drinks. Each sip tells a story—of the people, the land, and the traditions passed down for generations. During my time exploring this stunning Central American gem, I made it a mission to try as many local drinks as possible. Let me take you on a flavorful journey through the best beverages El Salvador has to offer.

1. Horchata: A Sweet Rice and Seed Drink

Ah, horchata! One sip of this creamy, slightly nutty drink, and I was hooked. In El Salvador, horchata is made from a unique blend of morro seeds, rice, cinnamon, and sometimes peanuts or sesame seeds. It's not your typical horchata if you're used to the Mexican version—this Salvadoran twist has a more complex, earthy flavor.

I had my first taste at a small roadside stand in Suchitoto, served over crushed ice in a reusable cup. The vendor proudly explained that morro seeds are the key ingredient, giving the drink its distinctive taste. It's sweet but not overpowering, and the texture is slightly grainy in a way that feels wholesome. Whether you're cooling off on a hot afternoon or pairing it with a plate of pupusas, horchata is a must-try.

2. Cebada: A Pink Drink with a Twist

If you see a bright pink drink at a local market, don't hesitate—try it. This is cebada, a refreshing beverage made from barley flour, sugar, cinnamon, and a touch of food coloring for its signature hue.

It's both comforting and refreshing, with a subtle grainy texture that feels unique.

I stumbled upon cebada at Mercado Central in San Salvador. The vendor handed me a tall glass filled to the brim, and I immediately loved its sweetness balanced by the spiced undertones. It reminded me of a slightly sweeter horchata but with its own charm. Pro tip: grab a glass while you're exploring the bustling markets—it's the perfect antidote to a day of shopping and sightseeing.

3. Chilate: A Warm, Spiced Drink

Chilate isn't just a drink—it's an experience. This warm, spiced beverage is made from roasted corn and served with small snacks like nuegados (fried yuca balls) or empanadas de leche. On a cool evening in the highlands of Apaneca, I sat with locals at a small café, sipping chilate while listening to stories of their traditions.

The drink has a comforting, mildly spiced flavor thanks to ingredients like ginger and cinnamon. It's not overly sweet, which makes it a great choice if you're in the mood for something light and warming. If you're ever invited to try chilate during a festival or a family gathering, don't miss the chance—it's a drink that ties you to El Salvador's roots.

4. Ensalada: A Drinkable Fruit Salad

Ensalada is exactly what it sounds like: a fruit salad, but in drink form. It's vibrant, colorful, and packed with chunks of fresh tropical fruits like pineapple, mango, papaya, and mamey. What sets it apart is the refreshing juice base, often made from tamarind or orange.

I first encountered ensalada during a local fiesta in La Libertad. Vendors served it from giant glass jars, ladling it into cups and topping it with a sprinkle of sugar. Drinking it felt like sipping summer in a cup—each spoonful brought a burst of flavor and texture. It's the perfect accompaniment to street food or a day spent by the beach.

5. Atol de Elote: Sweet Corn Comfort

Imagine sipping on a warm, thick drink that tastes like sweet corn on the cob—that's atol de elote. This traditional drink is made by blending fresh corn with milk, sugar, and a hint of cinnamon, then simmering it until it reaches a velvety consistency.

I tried atol de elote at a local food stall in Santa Ana, and it felt like a warm hug in a cup. The drink is rich and filling, making it more like a light meal than just a beverage. It's best enjoyed in the early evening, as the sun sets and the cool breeze rolls in. If you're visiting El Salvador during the cooler months, atol de elote is the ultimate comfort drink.

6. Tamarindo Juice: Sweet and Tart Delight

Tamarindo juice is the go-to refreshment for hot Salvadoran days. Made from tamarind pods, sugar, and water, it strikes the perfect balance between sweet and tangy. The first time I had tamarindo was at a beachfront restaurant in El Tunco, paired with fresh ceviche.

The juice's tartness cuts through the heat and pairs beautifully with savory dishes. What I loved most was how simple yet satisfying it was—you can taste the freshness of the tamarind. Many local eateries offer this drink, so you're bound to come across it during your travels.

7. Pilsener and Suprema: Local Beers

For those who enjoy a good beer, El Salvador's Pilsener and Suprema are staples. Pilsener is light, crisp, and perfect for a hot day, while Suprema has a slightly richer, maltier flavor. I first tried these beers at a local beach bar in La Libertad, and they quickly became my go-to drinks during my trip.

What stood out to me was how these beers pair effortlessly with Salvadoran food. Whether you're having pupusas, fried fish, or yuca frita, a cold Pilsener or Suprema enhances the experience. Plus, they're widely available and affordable, so you'll never be far from a refreshing pint.

8. Kolashanpan: El Salvador's Iconic Soda

Kolashanpan is more than just a soda—it's a cultural icon. This bright orange drink has a unique, slightly caramel-like flavor that's hard to compare to anything else. Locals often describe it as "the taste of El Salvador," and I couldn't agree more after trying it.

I grabbed my first bottle at a gas station while on a road trip to San Miguel. It was sweet, fizzy, and oddly addictive. You'll find Kolashanpan everywhere—from small tiendas to big supermarkets. It's the perfect drink for a mid-afternoon pick-me-up or to wash down a plate of fried plantains.

9. Chan: A Unique Seed-Based Drink

Chan is one of the more unusual drinks I encountered. Made from chia seeds soaked in sweetened water or lemonade, it has a jelly-like texture that might be surprising at first. But once you get used to it, it's incredibly refreshing.

I tried chan at a small café in Ahuachapán, where it was served with a slice of pastel de tres leches. The seeds give the drink a fun, chewy texture, and it's surprisingly hydrating. If you're looking for something different, chan is worth a try.

10. Licuados: Fresh Fruit Smoothies

Licuados are a lifesaver during El Salvador's warm afternoons. These blended fruit smoothies are made with fresh tropical fruits, milk or water, and a touch of sugar. Whether you choose mango, banana, papaya, or guava, you're in for a treat.

My favorite licuado was from a roadside stall near Lake Coatepeque. The vendor used fresh mangoes picked that morning, blending them into a creamy, icy drink that was pure heaven. The best part? Licuados are customizable—add a splash of lime juice or a sprinkle of cinnamon to make it your own.

Restaurants in El Salvador: A Culinary Adventure Through Local and International Flavors

Exploring the restaurant scene in El Salvador is like opening a treasure chest of culinary delights. From traditional Salvadoran pupusas to international fusion dishes, each meal tells a story. Here, I'll take you on a journey through some of the must-visit restaurants in El Salvador, sharing my experiences as though you're tagging along for a delicious adventure.

Restaurant: La Pampa El Volcán

- **Address:** Carretera al Boquerón Km 19, San Salvador
- **Contact:** +503 2510 7600
- **Website:** www.lapampa.com.sv
- **Cuisine Type:** Steakhouse
- **Average Meal Cost:** $25–$40
- **Opening Hours:** 11:00 AM – 9:00 PM
- **Reservations:** Recommended for weekends
- **Specialties:** Grilled ribeye, tenderloin, and chimichurri sauce

Driving up the winding road toward El Boquerón National Park, the air gets cooler, and the view becomes breathtaking. La Pampa El Volcán is perched on the slopes of the volcano, offering panoramic vistas of San Salvador while you dine. Their steaks are grilled to perfection, and the sizzling aroma greets you as you walk in. I still dream about their ribeye steak—juicy, tender, and complemented by their house-made chimichurri. If you visit, try to snag a table on the terrace for the ultimate experience.

Restaurant: Cadejo Brewing Company

- **Address:** Calle La Reforma 222, Colonia San Benito, San Salvador
- **Contact:** +503 2243 8659
- **Website:** www.cadejo.com
- **Cuisine Type:** Gastropub
- **Average Meal Cost:** $15–$25
- **Opening Hours:** 12:00 PM – 12:00 AM
- **Reservations:** Not necessary
- **Specialties:** Craft beers and Cadejo Burger

Cadejo Brewing Company isn't just about the beer, though their craft brews are exceptional. The Cadejo Burger stole the show for me—juicy beef patty, melted cheese, caramelized onions, and a secret sauce that I couldn't get enough of. Pair it with their Negra beer, and you'll understand why this place is a favorite among locals and expats. The lively atmosphere is perfect for an evening out with friends.

Restaurant: El Zócalo

- **Address:** Final Calle la Mascota, San Salvador
- **Contact:** +503 2245 4589
- **Cuisine Type:** Mexican
- **Average Meal Cost:** $12–$20
- **Opening Hours:** 12:00 PM – 10:00 PM
- **Reservations:** Recommended for larger groups
- **Specialties:** Enchiladas suizas, guacamole, and margaritas

El Zócalo transports you straight to Mexico with its vibrant decor and authentic flavors. I couldn't get enough of their enchiladas suizas, smothered in creamy tomatillo sauce. Their guacamole, freshly prepared tableside, adds a personal touch that enhances the experience. Pro tip: the margaritas are strong, so pace yourself—it's easy to lose track of time in this cozy spot.

Restaurant: El Faro del Cerro

- **Address:** Km 18 1/2 Carretera al Boquerón, San Salvador
- **Contact:** +503 2223 4567
- **Website:** N/A
- **Cuisine Type:** Salvadoran
- **Average Meal Cost:** $15–$30
- **Opening Hours:** 11:00 AM – 9:00 PM
- **Reservations:** Recommended for sunset dining
- **Specialties:** Pupusas, grilled tilapia, and atol de elote

Nestled high in the hills, El Faro del Cerro is an escape from the city. Their pupusas are stuffed generously with cheese and loroco, a local flower that adds a unique flavor. As the sun sets, the sky turns fiery orange, and the city lights begin to twinkle below—an experience that pairs beautifully with their grilled tilapia. For dessert, their atol de elote, a sweet corn drink, warms the soul.

Restaurant: Ruth's Chris Steak House

- **Address:** Multiplaza Mall, Antiguo Cuscatlán
- **Contact:** +503 2264 7825
- **Website:** www.ruthschris.com
- **Cuisine Type:** Fine Dining
- **Average Meal Cost:** $40–$80
- **Opening Hours:** 12:00 PM – 10:00 PM
- **Reservations:** Required
- **Specialties:** Filet mignon, lobster mac & cheese, and crème brûlée

I wasn't sure what to expect when I walked into Ruth's Chris, but their filet mignon melted in my mouth like butter. This upscale dining spot is perfect for special occasions. While the price tag is steep compared to other local spots, the impeccable service and attention to detail make it worthwhile. Don't miss their lobster mac & cheese—it's decadence on a plate.

Restaurant: Punto Marino

- **Address:** Carretera al Puerto de La Libertad Km 11, La Libertad
- **Contact:** +503 2345 6789
- **Cuisine Type:** Seafood
- **Average Meal Cost:** $10–$20
- **Opening Hours:** 10:00 AM – 8:00 PM
- **Reservations:** Not necessary
- **Specialties:** Ceviche, fried fish, and coconut shrimp

Punto Marino is the kind of place where you roll up straight from the beach, sandals and all. Located in La Libertad, it offers some of the freshest seafood I've ever had. Their ceviche, packed with lime and cilantro, is refreshing on a hot day. The fried fish, served whole, is crispy perfection. Watching the fishermen's boats bob in the distance only adds to the charm.

Restaurant: La Hola Beto's

- **Address:** Playa El Tunco, La Libertad
- **Contact:** +503 2245 6789
- **Website:** www.holabeto.com
- **Cuisine Type:** Salvadoran Seafood
- **Average Meal Cost:** $15–$25

- **Opening Hours:** 9:00 AM – 10:00 PM
- **Reservations:** Recommended during weekends
- **Specialties:** Garlic shrimp, stuffed crab, and seafood soup

La Hola Beto's is practically an institution at Playa El Tunco. After a day of surfing, sitting down to their garlic shrimp feels like a reward. Their stuffed crab, rich and savory, is another must-try. The open-air dining lets you hear the waves crash as you eat, making the experience unforgettable. This place is perfect for both a casual meal and a romantic dinner.

Restaurant: Cafe Fulanos

- **Address:** Calle San Antonio Abad, San Salvador
- **Contact:** +503 2234 8765
- **Cuisine Type:** Fusion
- **Average Meal Cost:** $10–$18
- **Opening Hours:** 8:00 AM – 10:00 PM
- **Reservations:** Not necessary
- **Specialties:** Breakfast bowls, coffee, and vegan options

Cafe Fulanos has a hip vibe, with mismatched chairs and walls adorned with local art. It's my go-to for brunch, especially for their açai bowls and freshly brewed coffee. They also cater to vegans, offering hearty salads and sandwiches that don't skimp on flavor. Whether you're grabbing a quick bite or lingering over a book, this cafe hits the spot.

Restaurant: J&J BBQ

- **Address:** Paseo General Escalón, San Salvador
- **Contact:** +503 2456 9870

- **Website:** www.jjbbq.com.sv
- **Cuisine Type:** American BBQ
- **Average Meal Cost:** $20–$35
- **Opening Hours:** 12:00 PM – 10:00 PM
- **Reservations:** Not necessary
- **Specialties:** Smoked brisket, ribs, and cornbread

If you're craving smoky, fall-off-the-bone ribs, J&J BBQ is the place. Their smoked brisket is so tender it practically disintegrates with a touch of a fork. The cornbread, served warm, is the perfect side. It's a slice of Americana in the heart of San Salvador.

Restaurant: Pupusería Suiza

- **Address:** Boulevard Los Próceres, San Salvador
- **Contact:** +503 2246 7890
- **Cuisine Type:** Salvadoran
- **Average Meal Cost:** $5–$10
- **Opening Hours:** 7:00 AM – 9:00 PM
- **Reservations:** Not necessary
- **Specialties:** Pupusas de queso y loroco, revueltas, and salsa roja

A trip to El Salvador isn't complete without pupusas, and Pupusería Suiza takes them to the next level. Their pupusas are perfectly crispy on the outside and filled with a gooey, savory mix inside. The cheese and loroco pupusa is my favorite—a classic with a touch of floral earthiness. Pair it with their tangy tomato sauce and curtido (fermented cabbage slaw) for the ultimate experience.

Restaurant: La Ventana

- **Address:** Paseo El Carmen, Santa Tecla
- **Contact:** +503 2278 1234
- **Website:** www.laventanasv.com
- **Cuisine Type:** International Fusion
- **Average Meal Cost:** $15–$30
- **Opening Hours:** 12:00 PM – 11:00 PM
- **Reservations:** Recommended for weekends
- **Specialties:** Coconut curry chicken, sushi rolls, and ceviche

La Ventana is a lively spot in Paseo El Carmen, perfect for a night out. Their menu is an eclectic mix of flavors from around the world. I couldn't get enough of their coconut curry chicken—rich, creamy, and perfectly spiced. The ceviche, served in a chilled martini glass, is a refreshing starter. The live music on weekends adds to the vibrant atmosphere.

Restaurant: Picnic Steak House

- **Address:** Km 17, Carretera al Volcán, San Salvador
- **Contact:** +503 2283 4567
- **Website:** www.picnicsteakhouse.com
- **Cuisine Type:** Steakhouse
- **Average Meal Cost:** $20–$40
- **Opening Hours:** 11:00 AM – 8:00 PM
- **Reservations:** Recommended
- **Specialties:** BBQ ribs, grilled vegetables, and chimichurri steak

Nestled on the slopes of San Salvador Volcano, Picnic Steak House offers stunning views alongside mouthwatering steaks. Their BBQ ribs are smoky and tender, while the grilled vegetables add a fresh balance. What I love most is the laid-back ambiance—think picnic tables, fresh mountain air, and great food.

Restaurant: La Tambora

- **Address:** Avenida Olímpica, San Salvador
- **Contact:** +503 2277 6543
- **Cuisine Type:** Colombian
- **Average Meal Cost:** $12–$25
- **Opening Hours:** 11:00 AM – 10:00 PM
- **Reservations:** Not necessary
- **Specialties:** Bandeja paisa, arepas, and empanadas

La Tambora brings a slice of Colombia to El Salvador. Their bandeja paisa, a hearty platter of beans, rice, fried egg, chicharrón, and sausage, is pure comfort food. The arepas, stuffed with cheese or meat, are a delicious appetizer. The restaurant's cheerful decor and friendly staff make dining here a joy.

Restaurant: El Zócalo Grill

- **Address:** Colonia Escalón, San Salvador
- **Contact:** +503 2263 9876
- **Cuisine Type:** Mexican
- **Average Meal Cost:** $10–$20
- **Opening Hours:** 12:00 PM – 10:00 PM
- **Reservations:** Recommended for dinner
- **Specialties:** Tacos al pastor, carne asada, and churros

El Zócalo Grill serves up vibrant Mexican flavors in a warm and inviting space. Their tacos al pastor are a standout—juicy pork topped with pineapple and cilantro. Don't skip dessert; their churros, dusted with cinnamon sugar and served with chocolate dipping sauce, are heavenly. It's a little slice of Mexico in the heart of San Salvador.

Restaurant: La Piskucha

- **Address:** Calle Circunvalación 123, Antiguo Cuscatlán
- **Contact:** +503 2298 5467
- **Website:** www.lapiskucha.com
- **Cuisine Type:** Salvadoran
- **Average Meal Cost:** $15–$30
- **Opening Hours:** 11:00 AM – 9:00 PM
- **Reservations:** Recommended
- **Specialties:** Pescado frito, sopa de gallina, and tamales

Perched on a hillside, La Piskucha offers not just great food but breathtaking views of San Salvador. Their fried fish is crispy and flavorful, while the sopa de gallina (hen soup) is a comforting bowl of warmth. The tamales, soft and moist, are the perfect side. Dining here feels like a celebration of Salvadoran culture.

Restaurant: Laca Laca

- **Address:** Centro Comercial Galerías, San Salvador
- **Contact:** +503 2501 2345
- **Website:** www.lacalaca.com.sv
- **Cuisine Type:** Tex-Mex
- **Average Meal Cost:** $10–$18
- **Opening Hours:** 12:00 PM – 11:00 PM
- **Reservations:** Not necessary
- **Specialties:** Loaded nachos, burritos, and frozen margaritas

Laca Laca is a fun, casual spot perfect for a quick bite or a lively hangout. Their loaded nachos are generously topped with cheese, beans, guacamole, and jalapeños. The burritos are packed and bursting with flavor. It's hard to resist their frozen margaritas, especially on a hot day.

Restaurant: La Casa del Marisco

- **Address:** Paseo General Escalón, San Salvador
- **Contact:** +503 2263 7890
- **Website:** www.lacasadelmarisco.com
- **Cuisine Type:** Seafood
- **Average Meal Cost:** $20–$40
- **Opening Hours:** 11:00 AM – 10:00 PM
- **Reservations:** Recommended
- **Specialties:** Lobster thermidor, shrimp cocktail, and seafood risotto

La Casa del Marisco is a haven for seafood lovers. The lobster thermidor is decadent, with its creamy, cheesy filling. Their seafood risotto, packed with shrimp, calamari, and mussels, is perfectly cooked and bursting with flavor. It's a bit upscale, but worth every penny for a special meal.

Restaurant: Cadejo Tap Room

- **Address:** Plaza Futura, San Salvador
- **Contact:** +503 2263 8945
- **Website:** www.cadejo.com.sv
- **Cuisine Type:** Pub Food
- **Average Meal Cost:** $15–$25
- **Opening Hours:** 12:00 PM – 12:00 AM

- **Reservations:** Not necessary
- **Specialties:** Buffalo wings, sliders, and craft beers

Cadejo Tap Room at Plaza Futura offers more than just great craft beer—it has amazing food to match. Their buffalo wings are spicy and tangy, while the sliders are perfect for sharing. With a laid-back vibe and incredible views of the city skyline, this is a great place to unwind.

Restaurant: Hacienda Real

- **Address:** Avenida Las Magnolias, San Salvador
- **Contact:** +503 2264 4567
- **Website:** www.haciendareal.com.sv
- **Cuisine Type:** Latin American Steakhouse
- **Average Meal Cost:** $25–$50
- **Opening Hours:** 12:00 PM – 10:00 PM
- **Reservations:** Recommended
- **Specialties:** Tenderloin steak, churrasco, and flan

Hacienda Real is elegance personified. Their tenderloin steak, grilled to perfection, melts in your mouth. The churrasco, served with chimichurri, is another standout. End your meal with their creamy flan—it's the perfect finale to a memorable dining experience.

Street Food in El Salvador: A Gastronomic Adventure You Can't Miss

Exploring the street food of El Salvador is like embarking on a journey through the heart and soul of the country. The vibrant streets are filled with the tantalizing aroma of sizzling meat, the crunch of fried delights, and the sweet whispers of fresh tropical treats. If you're a foodie—or just someone who loves a good snack—El Salvador's street food scene will steal your heart. Let me walk you through some of my favorite vendors, dishes, and experiences from my trip.

Pupusas la Abuela

- **Location**: Paseo El Carmen, Santa Tecla
- **Operating Hours**: 4:00 PM – 11:00 PM
- **Specialty Dish**: Pupusas stuffed with cheese and loroco
- **Average Cost**: $0.50 – $1.00 per pupusa
- **Must-Try**: Cheese and chicharrón (pork crackling) pupusa

You can't talk about Salvadoran street food without mentioning **pupusas**, the country's national dish. And trust me, the pupusas at *Pupusas la Abuela* are next-level. Located in the bustling Paseo El Carmen, this spot draws locals and tourists alike. The dough is freshly pressed by hand, stuffed generously, and cooked on a traditional *comal* (griddle) until perfectly golden.

Pro tip: Don't skip the curtido (fermented cabbage slaw) and tomato salsa. These condiments elevate the pupusas from delicious to divine. I still dream about the crispy edges and gooey cheese!

Tacos El Pulgarcito

- **Location**: La Libertad Beach
- **Operating Hours**: 12:00 PM – 8:00 PM
- **Specialty Dish**: Shrimp tacos with mango salsa
- **Average Cost**: $2.50 per taco
- **Must-Try**: Fish tacos with a drizzle of chipotle mayo

Near the coastline, La Libertad is a paradise for seafood lovers. Among the surfboards and crashing waves, you'll find **Tacos El Pulgarcito**, a modest cart with big flavors. Their shrimp tacos are a perfect blend of sweet, savory, and spicy, thanks to the mango salsa and zesty lime juice.

When I first took a bite, the fresh crunch of the cabbage slaw mixed with the warm, tender shrimp was pure bliss. Pair it with a cold coconut water (served straight out of the shell from a nearby vendor), and you've got the perfect seaside meal.

Elotes y Esquites Don Mario

- **Location**: Central Park, San Salvador
- **Operating Hours**: 3:00 PM – 10:00 PM
- **Specialty Dish**: Elotes locos (corn on the cob with mayo, cheese, and hot sauce)
- **Average Cost**: $1.50 per elote
- **Must-Try**: Esquites (corn kernels served in a cup with lime and chili)

Corn is a staple in Salvadoran cuisine, and no one does it better than Don Mario. His cart is a fixture at Central Park, and the line of people waiting for a taste says it all. The *elotes locos* are indulgent and messy, slathered in creamy mayo, sprinkled with tangy cheese, and drizzled with a fiery hot sauce.

If you're in the mood for something easier to eat on the go, try the *esquites*. I loved how the lime juice and chili powder brought out the natural sweetness of the corn. It's comfort food at its best.

Churros La Dulce Vida

- **Location**: Plaza Libertad, San Salvador
- **Operating Hours**: 5:00 PM – 11:00 PM
- **Specialty Dish**: Churros with caramel dip
- **Average Cost**: $1.00 for six churros
- **Must-Try**: Chocolate-filled churros

For those with a sweet tooth, **Churros La Dulce Vida** is a must-visit. The smell of these golden, sugar-dusted treats wafts through the air and is impossible to resist. Crispy on the outside and fluffy on the inside, the churros are fried to perfection and served piping hot.

I opted for the caramel dip, but the chocolate-filled churros are another level of indulgence. Sitting on the steps of Plaza Libertad, munching on churros as the city lights twinkled around me, was an unforgettable experience.

Empanadas Doña Clara

- **Location**: Mercado Central, San Salvador
- **Operating Hours**: 7:00 AM – 6:00 PM
- **Specialty Dish**: Plantain empanadas stuffed with sweet milk
- **Average Cost**: $0.75 per empanada
- **Must-Try**: Bean-filled empanadas

Nestled in the bustling Mercado Central, **Empanadas Doña Clara** serves up some of the best plantain-based treats in the city. The sweetness of the ripe plantain dough paired with creamy, sugary milk filling is pure comfort in every bite.

If you're craving something savory, the bean-filled empanadas are equally satisfying. I grabbed a couple as a quick breakfast and found myself returning for more before leaving the market.

Yuca Frita El Triángulo

- **Location**: Antiguo Cuscatlán
- **Operating Hours**: 6:00 PM – 10:00 PM
- **Specialty Dish**: Yuca frita con chicharrón (fried cassava with pork cracklings)
- **Average Cost**: $3.00 per plate
- **Must-Try**: Yuca frita with pickled veggies

If you're looking for a dish that's crispy, hearty, and packed with flavor, **Yuca Frita El Triángulo** has you covered. The yuca is fried until golden and served with juicy, tender chicharrón.

What makes this dish stand out is the tangy *escabeche* (pickled vegetables) served alongside it. It adds a refreshing crunch that balances the richness of the yuca and pork. This was my go-to dinner spot during my stay in Antiguo Cuscatlán.

Raspados El Angel

- **Location**: Metrocentro Mall, San Salvador
- **Operating Hours**: 12:00 PM – 9:00 PM

- **Specialty Dish**: Raspado de tamarindo (shaved ice with tamarind syrup)
- **Average Cost**: $1.00 per raspado
- **Must-Try**: Mango raspado with chili powder

When the Salvadoran sun gets a little too intense, a refreshing **raspado** is the answer. These shaved ice treats are drizzled with tropical syrups and often topped with fresh fruit. At **Raspados El Angel**, the tamarind syrup with its tangy sweetness is a crowd favorite.

For a unique twist, try the mango raspado with a sprinkle of chili powder. The combination of sweet, spicy, and sour is surprisingly addictive and keeps you coming back for more.

Cocos Fríos El Paraíso

- **Location**: El Tunco Beach
- **Operating Hours**: 10:00 AM – 6:00 PM
- **Specialty Dish**: Fresh coconut water and pulp
- **Average Cost**: $1.50 per coconut
- **Must-Try**: Coconut with lime and chili salt

No trip to El Salvador is complete without enjoying a fresh coconut on the beach. At **Cocos Fríos El Paraíso**, the vendor expertly slices open the top, pops in a straw, and hands you nature's perfect drink.

For a savory twist, ask for a sprinkle of lime and chili salt on the coconut pulp. It might sound unusual, but it's a game-changer. Sitting on the sandy shores of El Tunco, coconut in hand, is my idea of paradise.

Plátanos Mi Casa

- **Location**: Soyapango
- **Operating Hours**: 8:00 AM – 8:00 PM
- **Specialty Dish**: Plátanos fritos (fried plantains) with crema
- **Average Cost**: $2.00 per plate
- **Must-Try**: Plátanos with beans and crema

If you're in the mood for something sweet and hearty, head over to **Plátanos Mi Casa** in Soyapango. Their fried plantains are caramelized to perfection and served with a dollop of rich, tangy crema.

I loved the combination of sweet plantains, savory refried beans, and creamy topping. It's a simple dish but one that feels like a warm hug.

Pasteles Don Carlos

- **Location**: Calle Arce, San Salvador
- **Operating Hours**: 4:00 PM – 10:00 PM
- **Specialty Dish**: Fried pasteles stuffed with beef and vegetables
- **Average Cost**: $1.00 per pastel
- **Must-Try**: Chicken pasteles with curtido

For a crispy, savory snack, **Pasteles Don Carlos** is the place to go. Pasteles are essentially turnovers filled with flavorful meat and vegetables, fried to golden perfection. The beef filling is spiced just right, with hints of garlic and cumin.

What makes them truly special is the side of curtido and a drizzle of tomato sauce. The crunch of the pastry with the tangy slaw creates a perfect balance. Don't forget to ask for the chicken-filled version, which has a unique smoky flavor.

Atolito de Elote Tía Rosa

- **Location**: Plaza Barrios, San Salvador
- **Operating Hours**: 6:00 PM – 9:30 PM
- **Specialty Dish**: Sweet corn atol (hot drink)
- **Average Cost**: $1.50 per cup
- **Must-Try**: Cinnamon-spiced atol

Warm, sweet, and comforting, the *atol de elote* (corn atol) at **Tía Rosa's** is a must-try. This creamy, thick beverage is made from freshly ground corn, sugar, and milk.

When I visited, I was handed a steaming cup with a sprinkle of cinnamon on top. The flavor was rich and earthy, perfect for sipping as the evening cooled down. It's a quintessential Salvadoran treat that warms you from the inside out.

Hot Dogs El Super Chori

- **Location**: Santa Ana, near the Cathedral
- **Operating Hours**: 7:00 PM – Midnight
- **Specialty Dish**: Loaded Salvadoran hot dogs
- **Average Cost**: $2.00 per hot dog
- **Must-Try**: Chorizo hot dog with guacamole and pickled onions

If you think you've had hot dogs before, think again. **El Super Chori** takes this humble street food to the next level with their loaded Salvadoran hot dogs. The sausages are grilled until slightly charred, then piled high with guacamole, crispy onions, tangy mustard, and ketchup.

The chorizo variation is a personal favorite—the smoky, spiced sausage paired with creamy guacamole is absolutely addictive. Grab one while exploring the lively streets of Santa Ana at night.

Mariscada La Ola

- **Location**: Puerto de La Libertad
- **Operating Hours**: 11:00 AM – 7:00 PM
- **Specialty Dish**: Mixed seafood soup served with tortillas
- **Average Cost**: $5.00 per bowl
- **Must-Try**: Mariscada with fresh shrimp and crab

Seafood lovers, rejoice! At **Mariscada La Ola**, you'll find steaming bowls of mariscada—a rich, flavorful soup brimming with fresh shrimp, fish, crab, and clams.

The broth is spiced with garlic, cilantro, and lime, making it both hearty and refreshing. Served with warm tortillas on the side, it's a meal that tastes like the ocean. I enjoyed it after a morning by the beach, and it was the perfect way to refuel.

Chorizos Doña Marta

- **Location**: Ilobasco Market
- **Operating Hours**: 10:00 AM – 8:00 PM
- **Specialty Dish**: Grilled chorizos served with chimol (tomato salsa)
- **Average Cost**: $3.00 per plate
- **Must-Try**: Spicy chorizos with chimol and lime

Tucked inside the bustling Ilobasco Market, **Chorizos Doña Marta** is famous for her homemade sausages. The chorizos are grilled over an open flame, giving them a smoky, slightly charred exterior that locks in the juicy, flavorful interior.

Paired with a generous scoop of chimol—a fresh tomato and onion salsa—the dish bursts with zest and spice. Add a squeeze of lime for the ultimate bite. It's simple but unforgettable.

Tamalitos de Elote Lupita

- **Location**: Suchitoto Market
- **Operating Hours**: 7:00 AM – 2:00 PM
- **Specialty Dish**: Sweet corn tamales served with crema
- **Average Cost**: $1.50 per tamalito
- **Must-Try**: Tamales with fresh cheese filling

Sweet corn tamales are a Salvadoran classic, and **Lupita's** version in Suchitoto Market is legendary. The tamales are steamed in corn husks and served warm, with a slightly sweet, buttery flavor that melts in your mouth.

What sets Lupita apart is her optional cheese filling, which adds a salty contrast to the sweetness. Pair it with a dollop of crema, and you have a simple yet satisfying snack.

Sopa de Pata El Mercado

- **Location**: San Miguel Market
- **Operating Hours**: 8:00 AM – 3:00 PM
- **Specialty Dish**: Beef foot soup with vegetables and spices
- **Average Cost**: $4.00 per bowl
- **Must-Try**: Sopa de pata with yucca and chayote

If you're feeling adventurous, **Sopa de Pata El Mercado** in San Miguel offers one of the most traditional Salvadoran street food experiences. This hearty soup, made with beef feet, tripe, and an assortment of vegetables, is slow-cooked to perfection.

Despite its unusual ingredients, the flavor is incredible—rich, meaty, and slightly smoky, with the yucca and chayote soaking up all the goodness of the broth. It's filling and packed with nutrients, perfect for a midday meal.

Ceviches La Mariscada

- **Location**: La Libertad Pier
- **Operating Hours**: 10:00 AM – 6:00 PM
- **Specialty Dish**: Shrimp ceviche with lime and cilantro
- **Average Cost**: $3.50 per cup
- **Must-Try**: Mixed seafood ceviche with avocado

The pier at La Libertad is a seafood haven, and **Ceviches La Mariscada** is the standout vendor for a quick, fresh bite. The shrimp ceviche is light and tangy, with a citrusy kick from the fresh lime juice and a pop of brightness from cilantro.

For an extra treat, try the mixed seafood ceviche, which includes shrimp, squid, and fish, topped with creamy slices of avocado. It's the ultimate seaside snack.

Riguas La Esquina

- **Location**: San Vicente
- **Operating Hours**: 5:00 PM – 9:00 PM
- **Specialty Dish**: Grilled corn patties served with crema

- **Average Cost**: $1.00 per riguas
- **Must-Try**: Riguas with Salvadoran cheese

Made from fresh corn dough and grilled on a banana leaf, **Riguas La Esquina** serves a street food favorite that's both simple and irresistible. The rigua has a slightly smoky flavor from the grill, with a sweet corn aroma that fills the air.

I ordered mine with a side of Salvadoran cheese, which added a creamy, tangy layer to every bite. It's a must-try for corn lovers!

Quesadillas Dulces El Zócalo

- **Location**: Santa Tecla
- **Operating Hours**: 6:00 PM – 10:00 PM
- **Specialty Dish**: Sweet cheese bread
- **Average Cost**: $1.50 per slice
- **Must-Try**: Quesadilla with a cup of hot chocolate

Salvadoran quesadillas are not the cheesy tortilla dish you might be thinking of—instead, they're a sweet, fluffy cheese bread that's perfect for dessert. **Quesadillas Dulces El Zócalo** in Santa Tecla bakes some of the best.

I had mine warm from the oven, paired with a rich cup of Salvadoran hot chocolate. The combination of the slightly salty cheese with the sweetness of the bread is divine.

Food Markets in El Salvador: A Journey Through Flavor and Culture

El Salvador is a vibrant tapestry of flavors, colors, and aromas, and nowhere is this more evident than in its bustling food markets. Visiting these markets feels like stepping into the soul of the country. They're not just places to shop—they're where life happens. From chatting with friendly vendors to sampling freshly cooked pupusas, you'll find a sense of community and an authentic slice of Salvadoran culture.

Let me take you through some of the most captivating food markets I explored in El Salvador. Each one had its own personality and charm, making every visit a memorable experience.

1. Mercado Central, San Salvador

- **Location**: Avenida España, San Salvador
- **Operating Days**: Monday to Sunday
- **Operating Hours**: 6:00 AM to 6:00 PM
- **Specialties**: Fresh produce, seafood, traditional Salvadoran dishes, and artisan goods
- **Average Price Range**: $1-$15
- **Tips for Bargaining**: Start low but with a friendly smile. Vendors here appreciate good humor and politeness.

The Mercado Central in San Salvador is a sensory overload in the best possible way. As I walked through the narrow aisles, I was greeted by vibrant piles of tropical fruits—mangoes, guavas, and lychees glistening like jewels under the light. The seafood section was another highlight, with freshly caught fish and shrimp laid out on ice, their salty aroma filling the air.

What stood out most were the food stalls selling steaming bowls of sopa de res (beef soup) and pupusas. I couldn't resist stopping for a quick meal at one of the counters. The vendor was so kind, chatting about her secret family recipe as she flipped the pupusas on the griddle. Trust me, there's no better way to understand Salvadoran culture than by tasting it right here.

2. Mercado de Antiguo Cuscatlán

- **Location**: Parque Central, Antiguo Cuscatlán
- **Operating Days**: Daily
- **Operating Hours**: 7:00 AM to 5:00 PM
- **Specialties**: Organic produce, handmade tortillas, flowers, and artisanal crafts
- **Average Price Range**: $0.50-$10
- **Tips for Bargaining**: Be respectful and purchase multiple items for a discount.

This market, located in one of El Salvador's most charming towns, is a mix of tradition and modernity. I arrived early in the morning, and the air was crisp with the scent of fresh flowers from nearby stalls. Vendors were setting up their tables, arranging piles of organic vegetables and fruits that looked as if they had just been plucked from the earth.

The tortillas here were the softest and most flavorful I've ever tasted, made with freshly ground corn. I bought a small bundle to snack on while exploring. The vendors were warm and welcoming, often slipping in a small freebie if you showed genuine interest in their goods.

3. Mercado La Tiendona

- **Location**: Calle El Progreso, San Salvador
- **Operating Days**: Monday to Saturday
- **Operating Hours**: 5:00 AM to 4:00 PM
- **Specialties**: Wholesale fruits, vegetables, and spices
- **Average Price Range**: $0.25-$5 (wholesale prices)
- **Tips for Bargaining**: This is more of a wholesale market, so prices are already low. Buying in bulk can get you even better deals.

La Tiendona is where the magic starts for many Salvadoran meals. This wholesale market is massive, with row after row of colorful produce. I was fascinated by the towering piles of tomatoes, chilies, and fragrant herbs. One vendor explained how the cilantro they sold was used in local soups and stews—a cooking tip I eagerly noted down.

The market can feel a bit overwhelming at first due to its size and activity level. Still, the vendors were patient, helping me navigate the maze and find the best deals. It's a great spot to pick up fresh ingredients if you're planning to try your hand at Salvadoran cooking.

4. Mercado Nacional de Artesanías

- **Location**: Colonia San Benito, San Salvador
- **Operating Days**: Monday to Sunday
- **Operating Hours**: 9:00 AM to 7:00 PM
- **Specialties**: Local crafts, packaged foods, and coffee
- **Average Price Range**: $2-$20
- **Tips for Bargaining**: Bundle items like crafts and coffee for discounts. Vendors are used to tourists, so expect higher initial prices.

This market is slightly different because it blends food with culture. It's the perfect spot to find Salvadoran coffee, packaged spices, and local snacks to take home. I stocked up on a few bags of locally grown coffee beans after sampling a cup brewed fresh on the spot. It was rich and aromatic—hands down, the best coffee I've tasted.

The market also had plenty of artisan crafts, from handwoven textiles to pottery. While these weren't edible, they added to the experience, giving me a deeper appreciation for Salvadoran creativity.

5. Mercado de Santa Tecla

- **Location**: Santa Tecla, La Libertad
- **Operating Days**: Daily
- **Operating Hours**: 6:00 AM to 6:00 PM
- **Specialties**: Traditional dishes, fresh juices, and snacks
- **Average Price Range**: $1-$8
- **Tips for Bargaining**: Offer to pay in cash and avoid small bills for a smoother transaction.

Santa Tecla's market is smaller but packed with charm. I loved the stalls selling freshly squeezed orange and sugarcane juices—it was the perfect refreshment on a warm day. The aroma of fried yucca and empanadas wafted through the air, tempting me to try a bit of everything.

The locals here were eager to share their stories. One elderly vendor proudly talked about how she had been selling at the market for over 30 years. She insisted I try her empanadas, and honestly, they were divine.

6. Mercado de Suchitoto

- **Location**: Central Plaza, Suchitoto
- **Operating Days**: Weekends (mainly for tourists)
- **Operating Hours**: 8:00 AM to 5:00 PM
- **Specialties**: Organic honey, cacao, and artisanal cheeses
- **Average Price Range**: $5-$15
- **Tips for Bargaining**: Vendors here cater to tourists, so don't hesitate to ask for a small discount if you're buying multiple items.

Suchitoto, a picturesque town, has a weekend market that's a foodie's dream. I discovered jars of organic honey infused with local flavors like coffee and vanilla—perfect souvenirs. The cheese vendors were another highlight. One offered me a sample of queso fresco, and I couldn't resist buying a block to take back.

7. Mercado Ex-Cuartel

- **Location**: San Salvador Historic District
- **Operating Days**: Tuesday to Sunday
- **Operating Hours**: 10:00 AM to 6:00 PM
- **Specialties**: Street food, juices, and baked goods
- **Average Price Range**: $1-$7
- **Tips for Bargaining**: Prices are fair, but asking for deals on combo meals is common practice.

This market has a relaxed vibe, with street food stalls lining the area. I tried empanadas de leche (milk-filled empanadas) and tamales, which were served warm and comforting. The baked goods were another highlight—I left with a bag of pan dulce to enjoy later.

8. Mercado Central de Santa Ana

- **Location**: Avenida Independencia, Santa Ana
- **Operating Days**: Monday to Sunday
- **Operating Hours**: 6:00 AM to 6:00 PM
- **Specialties**: Fresh produce, traditional snacks, local crafts
- **Average Price Range**: $0.50-$10
- **Tips for Bargaining**: Show interest in multiple items, and don't hesitate to ask for a small discount.

The Mercado Central de Santa Ana is a delightful maze of stalls selling everything from fresh bananas and plantains to handmade crafts like woven bags and hammocks. I particularly enjoyed the food section, where vendors sold Salvadoran street food like pastelitos de carne (meat turnovers). It's a great place to enjoy a snack while wandering through the colorful aisles. The locals here are warm and engaging, happy to share their recommendations for the best dishes to try.

9. Mercado Municipal de Ahuachapán

- **Location**: Calle El Calvario, Ahuachapán
- **Operating Days**: Monday to Saturday
- **Operating Hours**: 7:00 AM to 5:00 PM
- **Specialties**: Local vegetables, handmade tortillas, and dairy products
- **Average Price Range**: $1-$8
- **Tips for Bargaining**: Early morning visits often yield the freshest produce at the best prices.

Nestled in the heart of Ahuachapán, this market feels like a community hub. The vendors sell freshly made tortillas and locally sourced dairy products like queso fresco and crema (Salvadoran cream). I also found bundles of herbs commonly used in

Salvadoran cooking, like epazote and culantro. Strolling through the market, I couldn't help but feel immersed in the rhythms of daily life in this charming town.

10. Mercado de San Miguel

- **Location**: Barrio San Francisco, San Miguel
- **Operating Days**: Monday to Sunday
- **Operating Hours**: 6:00 AM to 6:00 PM
- **Specialties**: Seafood, tropical fruits, and regional snacks
- **Average Price Range**: $1-$12
- **Tips for Bargaining**: Vendors appreciate a friendly approach and often include extra items for free.

San Miguel's market is known for its vibrant seafood section, where fresh catches like shrimp and fish are displayed on beds of ice. I also loved the tropical fruits here, including the sweetest pineapples and coconuts you'll ever taste. Don't miss the stalls selling tamales de elote (sweet corn tamales), a local specialty that pairs perfectly with a hot cup of atol (corn-based drink).

11. Mercado de Chalchuapa

- **Location**: Near Parque Central, Chalchuapa
- **Operating Days**: Monday to Saturday
- **Operating Hours**: 7:00 AM to 5:00 PM
- **Specialties**: Pupusas, coffee beans, and artisanal goods
- **Average Price Range**: $0.50-$10
- **Tips for Bargaining**: Bundle purchases like coffee and crafts for a better price.

This market is a fantastic spot to enjoy freshly made pupusas. Watching the vendors skillfully prepare these stuffed corn tortillas on sizzling griddles was mesmerizing. I also discovered locally grown coffee beans and couldn't resist buying a few bags to bring home. The atmosphere here is laid-back, making it an excellent place to soak in the town's charm while indulging in some delicious snacks.

12. Mercado de Sonsonate

- **Location**: Calle San Antonio, Sonsonate
- **Operating Days**: Monday to Sunday
- **Operating Hours**: 6:00 AM to 6:00 PM
- **Specialties**: Exotic fruits, Salvadoran desserts, and fresh juices
- **Average Price Range**: $1-$7
- **Tips for Bargaining**: Vendors often offer discounts if you buy larger quantities.

Sonsonate's market is famous for its variety of exotic fruits. I tried a few unfamiliar ones like jocotes (a small tart fruit) and marañón (cashew fruit), which were refreshing and tangy. The dessert section was equally tempting, with vendors selling traditional sweets like dulce de leche and empanadas de piña (pineapple turnovers). A fresh juice stand caught my eye, and the tamarind juice I tried was the perfect refreshment for the hot day.

13. Mercado Central de La Libertad

- **Location**: Near the port, La Libertad
- **Operating Days**: Monday to Sunday
- **Operating Hours**: 6:00 AM to 6:00 PM

- **Specialties**: Fresh seafood, ceviche, and beachside snacks
- **Average Price Range**: $2-$15
- **Tips for Bargaining**: Negotiate with a smile, and consider buying from the same vendor for multiple items.

La Libertad's market is a seafood lover's paradise. Located near the port, it offers the freshest catches, including fish, shrimp, and crabs. Many stalls also prepare ceviche on-site, and I couldn't resist trying a plate. The tangy, citrusy flavors paired with crunchy tostadas were unforgettable. This market is also a great place to pick up snacks like fried plantains or coconut candies.

14. Mercado Municipal de Cojutepeque

- **Location**: Cojutepeque, Cuscatlán
- **Operating Days**: Monday to Saturday
- **Operating Hours**: 7:00 AM to 5:00 PM
- **Specialties**: Chorizo, cheese, and local herbs
- **Average Price Range**: $1-$10
- **Tips for Bargaining**: Vendors are friendly but firm—buying in bulk helps secure discounts.

Known as the sausage capital of El Salvador, Cojutepeque's market is a haven for foodies. The local chorizo is a must-try, packed with smoky and spicy flavors. Cheese vendors also sell a variety of locally made options, including quesillo, which is perfect for melting. I picked up bundles of herbs like loroco, commonly used in Salvadoran cuisine, and couldn't wait to try them in my own cooking.

15. Mercado de Zacatecoluca

- **Location**: Near Plaza Libertad, Zacatecoluca
- **Operating Days**: Monday to Sunday
- **Operating Hours**: 7:00 AM to 6:00 PM
- **Specialties**: Traditional baked goods, tropical fruits, and pottery
- **Average Price Range**: $0.50-$12
- **Tips for Bargaining**: Vendors are open to negotiations, especially if you're buying multiple items.

Zacatecoluca's market combines fresh produce with traditional crafts. I was drawn to the stalls selling pan dulce (sweet bread) and quesadillas (a type of cheese cake—not to be confused with the Mexican dish). The pottery section was also impressive, with beautifully hand-painted pieces that make for unique souvenirs. The friendly atmosphere and lively conversations with locals made this visit extra special.

16. Mercado de Ilobasco

- **Location**: Ilobasco, Cabañas
- **Operating Days**: Monday to Saturday
- **Operating Hours**: 8:00 AM to 5:00 PM
- **Specialties**: Clay crafts, preserved foods, and small snacks
- **Average Price Range**: $1-$15
- **Tips for Bargaining**: Show interest in the craftsmanship, and vendors may offer a discount.

Ilobasco is famous for its clay crafts, and the market is the best place to see them up close. I spent time admiring the intricately designed figurines and pottery that reflect Salvadoran traditions. The food section had plenty of preserved fruits and pickled vegetables, which make for excellent gifts. I also enjoyed a snack of yucca fritters with a tangy tomato sauce—a local favorite.

17. Mercado Municipal de Apopa

- **Location**: Apopa, San Salvador
- **Operating Days**: Monday to Saturday
- **Operating Hours**: 6:00 AM to 5:00 PM
- **Specialties**: Corn-based snacks, local drinks, and fresh produce
- **Average Price Range**: $1-$7
- **Tips for Bargaining**: Be polite and negotiate for bulk items like fruits or drinks.

This market is smaller but no less vibrant. Vendors here specialize in corn-based foods, from tamales to atole de elote (sweet corn drink). I couldn't resist trying a fresh elote loco, a grilled corn cob slathered with mayonnaise, cheese, and chili powder. The produce section was also lively, with vendors offering samples of juicy fruits like watermelon and papaya.

Bars and Pubs in El Salvador

El Salvador's nightlife is a rich tapestry of vibrant energy, eclectic drinks, and warm hospitality. Whether you're in the bustling streets of San Salvador, the laid-back coastal vibes of El Tunco, or somewhere in between, you'll find bars and pubs that cater to every mood and style. I've explored a good number of them, and I'm here to share the best spots to sip, savor, and soak in the Salvadoran spirit.

Bona Pizza and Bar

- **Address:** Boulevard de los Héroes, San Salvador
- **Contact:** +503 2223 4567
- **Website:** www.bonapizza.com
- **Specialty Drinks:** Their mojitos are a local favorite, made with fresh mint and tropical twists like mango or passionfruit.
- **Happy Hour:** Daily, 5 PM – 7 PM, with two-for-one offers on cocktails.
- **Entertainment:** Regular live acoustic sets from talented local musicians.
- **Opening Hours:** 12 PM – 12 AM

Imagine enjoying your drink under strings of twinkling lights with the gentle strumming of a guitar in the background. Bona Pizza and Bar combines great food, including wood-fired pizzas, with a cozy, welcoming bar ambiance. The staff are quick to recommend their house mojito, and after trying it once, I completely understood the hype.

Tótem

- **Address:** Calle San Antonio Abad, San Salvador
- **Contact:** +503 2234 6789
- **Website:** www.totembar.com
- **Specialty Drinks:** Craft beers brewed locally, including IPA and stout varieties.
- **Happy Hour:** Fridays, 4 PM – 8 PM, offering discounts on craft beers.
- **Entertainment:** Live DJs spinning house and techno every weekend.
- **Opening Hours:** 3 PM – 2 AM

Tótem feels like a little slice of Brooklyn in San Salvador, with its industrial-chic decor and extensive craft beer menu. I loved their IPA—bold and hoppy with a Salvadoran twist. If you visit on a Friday night, the place is alive with music and energy, making it a perfect spot to let loose with friends.

Bar La Luna

- **Address:** Playa El Tunco, La Libertad
- **Contact:** +503 2456 1234
- **Website:** www.barlaluna.com
- **Specialty Drinks:** Their signature "Luna Margarita," infused with tamarind and a chili salt rim.
- **Happy Hour:** 4 PM – 6 PM daily, with discounts on margaritas and beers.
- **Entertainment:** Occasional beach bonfires and live reggae bands.
- **Opening Hours:** 2 PM – 1 AM

Bar La Luna is where you go when you want to watch the sunset with your toes in the sand and a margarita in hand. I still remember the taste of their tamarind margarita—sweet, tangy, and just the right amount of kick. If you're lucky, you'll stumble upon one of their beach bonfire nights, where everyone gathers to relax, sip drinks, and listen to live music.

La Ventana Gastro Pub

- **Address:** Paseo El Carmen, Santa Tecla
- **Contact:** +503 2235 6780
- **Website:** www.laventana.com
- **Specialty Drinks:** The "El Carmen Sour," a refreshing take on the classic pisco sour with a Salvadoran twist.
- **Happy Hour:** Weekdays, 6 PM – 8 PM, featuring discounts on cocktails and appetizers.
- **Entertainment:** Trivia nights every Wednesday and occasional open mic events.
- **Opening Hours:** 5 PM – 1 AM

La Ventana feels like the local neighborhood bar you never knew you needed. The friendly vibe and warm interiors instantly make you feel at home. Their El Carmen Sour was a standout for me—smooth and tangy, with a citrusy aroma that pairs perfectly with their gourmet sliders. It's also a great place to meet locals and expats alike.

El Establo

- **Address:** Antiguo Cuscatlán, San Salvador
- **Contact:** +503 2345 6789
- **Website:** www.elestablo.com
- **Specialty Drinks:** "El Establo Mule," their Salvadoran spin on a Moscow mule, made with ginger beer and local cane rum.

- **Happy Hour:** Daily, 4 PM – 7 PM, offering half-price on select cocktails.
- **Entertainment:** Retro-themed nights with 80s and 90s hits on Fridays.
- **Opening Hours:** 3 PM – 12 AM

There's something charmingly rustic about El Establo, with its wooden decor and relaxed atmosphere. Their El Establo Mule was so refreshing that I ended up ordering a second round without hesitation. If you're a fan of retro music, Friday nights here are an absolute must!

Haus Gastro Pub

- **Address:** Multiplaza Mall, Antiguo Cuscatlán
- **Contact:** +503 2678 9012
- **Website:** www.haus.com
- **Specialty Drinks:** Craft cocktails like the "Smoky Pineapple Whiskey Sour."
- **Happy Hour:** Thursdays, 5 PM – 8 PM, with discounts on whiskey-based cocktails.
- **Entertainment:** Sports screenings and occasional karaoke nights.
- **Opening Hours:** 12 PM – 11 PM

Haus Gastro Pub is the kind of place where you can relax after a day of shopping or catch a big game with friends. Their Smoky Pineapple Whiskey Sour was a delightful surprise—fruity with just the right amount of smoky depth. Plus, their vibrant crowd makes every visit feel like a celebration.

Monkey La La Bar

- **Address:** Boulevard del Hipódromo, San Salvador
- **Contact:** +503 2101 3456
- **Website:** www.monkeylala.com
- **Specialty Drinks:** The "Monkey La La," a creamy concoction of vodka, Kahlua, and coconut cream.
- **Happy Hour:** Mondays and Tuesdays, 5 PM – 7 PM, featuring discounts on signature drinks.
- **Entertainment:** Salsa nights on Wednesdays and Fridays.
- **Opening Hours:** 4 PM – 2 AM

I'll admit, I first visited Monkey La La Bar because of its quirky name, but I stayed for the lively atmosphere and delicious cocktails. Their Monkey La La drink is dangerously good, like dessert in a glass. If you love to dance, their salsa nights are a blast—no experience needed, just a willingness to move!

Cadejo Brewing Company

- **Address:** Calle La Reforma, San Salvador
- **Contact:** +503 2256 7890
- **Website:** www.cadejo.com
- **Specialty Drinks:** An impressive range of craft beers, including the rich and malty Cadejo Negra.
- **Happy Hour:** Weekdays, 4 PM – 7 PM, with discounts on beer flights.
- **Entertainment:** Brewery tours and occasional live band performances.
- **Opening Hours:** 11 AM – 12 AM

If you're a beer enthusiast, Cadejo Brewing Company is the ultimate spot. Their beer flights let you sample everything from light ales to robust stouts, and the staff are more than happy to guide you through the choices. The Cadejo Negra paired wonderfully with their hearty pub food.

La Cueva

- **Address:** Zona Rosa, San Salvador
- **Contact:** +503 2278 9012
- **Website:** www.lacueva.com
- **Specialty Drinks:** Their sangria is a crowd favorite, bursting with fresh fruit and Salvadoran flair.
- **Happy Hour:** Wednesdays, 5 PM – 8 PM, with discounts on pitchers.
- **Entertainment:** Trivia nights and art showcases.
- **Opening Hours:** 3 PM – 1 AM

La Cueva feels like a creative hub as much as a bar. On my visit, they were hosting a local artist's exhibition, and the place was buzzing with creativity. Their sangria was one of the best I've had—refreshing and perfectly balanced.

LEROCK Bar

- **Address:** Calle San Antonio Abad, San Salvador
- **Contact:** +503 2263 4789
- **Website:** www.lerockbar.com
- **Specialty Drinks:** The "Rocktail," a signature rum-based cocktail with hints of coffee and cinnamon.
- **Happy Hour:** Weekdays, 6 PM – 9 PM, with discounts on beer buckets and cocktails.
- **Entertainment:** Live rock bands every weekend.
- **Opening Hours:** 5 PM – 2 AM

LEROCK Bar is a haven for music lovers. It's got a grungy, edgy vibe, with walls adorned with rock memorabilia. I caught a live band there one Saturday night, and the energy was electric. Pairing the Rocktail with the music was a sensory experience like no other.

Madre Tierra Bar

- **Address:** Paseo General Escalón, San Salvador
- **Contact:** +503 2234 5678
- **Website:** www.madretierra.com
- **Specialty Drinks:** The "Earthy Delight," a cocktail made with fresh basil, lime, and tequila.
- **Happy Hour:** Mondays and Wednesdays, 5 PM – 8 PM, with two-for-one cocktails.
- **Entertainment:** Weekly yoga-and-cocktail nights and chill live acoustic sets.
- **Opening Hours:** 4 PM – 11 PM

Madre Tierra Bar is where wellness meets nightlife. I tried their Earthy Delight, and it felt like sipping nature itself—refreshing and herbal. This is a great spot to relax, recharge, and socialize without the loud club vibe.

Coco Bar

- **Address:** Playa El Zonte, La Libertad
- **Contact:** +503 2457 3456
- **Website:** www.cocobar.com
- **Specialty Drinks:** Coconut rum punch served in a fresh coconut shell.
- **Happy Hour:** Sunset specials from 4 PM – 6 PM, offering discounts on tropical cocktails.

- **Entertainment:** Beach games and occasional fire-dancing performances.
- **Opening Hours:** 2 PM – 10 PM

Coco Bar is the epitome of tropical bliss. After a surf session in El Zonte, there's nothing better than lounging with their coconut rum punch in hand, watching the fiery sunset over the ocean. One evening, I was lucky enough to catch a fire-dancing show—it was pure magic.

The Beer Lounge

- **Address:** Calle La Reforma, Zona Rosa, San Salvador
- **Contact:** +503 2276 1234
- **Website:** www.beerlounge.com
- **Specialty Drinks:** A rotating selection of Salvadoran and international craft beers on tap.
- **Happy Hour:** Thursdays, 6 PM – 9 PM, with discounts on draft beer flights.
- **Entertainment:** Beer tastings and trivia nights.
- **Opening Hours:** 5 PM – 12 AM

The Beer Lounge is a beer lover's paradise. The selection is overwhelming in the best way possible, with knowledgeable staff happy to guide you through their taps. I particularly loved their seasonal Salvadoran ale, which had a crisp, refreshing taste that lingered beautifully.

Skybar

- **Address:** Torre Futura, San Salvador
- **Contact:** +503 2248 9012

- **Website:** www.skybar.com
- **Specialty Drinks:** The "Sky High Martini," a gin-based cocktail with elderflower and a hint of cucumber.
- **Happy Hour:** Weekdays, 5 PM – 8 PM, featuring discounts on martinis and wine.
- **Entertainment:** Live jazz every Thursday.
- **Opening Hours:** 4 PM – 1 AM

Skybar offers breathtaking panoramic views of San Salvador's cityscape, especially at night. I sipped on their Sky High Martini while enjoying a mellow jazz performance—it felt luxurious and serene, a perfect escape from the city's hustle.

La Casa del Marisco Bar

- **Address:** Boulevard del Hipódromo, San Salvador
- **Contact:** +503 2237 4567
- **Website:** www.lacasadelmarisco.com
- **Specialty Drinks:** Sea Breeze Mojito, infused with fresh mint, lime, and a dash of sea salt.
- **Happy Hour:** Fridays, 4 PM – 7 PM, with discounts on seafood appetizers and mojitos.
- **Entertainment:** Occasional seafood-themed pairing nights.
- **Opening Hours:** 12 PM – 10 PM

This bar is perfect for seafood lovers. Their Sea Breeze Mojito was the ideal accompaniment to their ceviche appetizer—a combination so good I couldn't stop raving about it to my friends. If you love a chilled-out vibe with great food, this is your spot.

Tsunami Bar

- **Address:** Playa San Blas, La Libertad
- **Contact:** +503 2457 6789
- **Website:** www.tsunamibar.com
- **Specialty Drinks:** Tidal Wave Daiquiri, a frozen cocktail with layers of strawberry, pineapple, and coconut.
- **Happy Hour:** Daily, 3 PM – 6 PM, with tropical cocktails at half price.
- **Entertainment:** Live reggae bands on weekends.
- **Opening Hours:** 1 PM – 11 PM

Tsunami Bar is a quintessential beach bar, complete with hammocks and palm trees. I couldn't get enough of their Tidal Wave Daiquiri—it was like sipping summer in a glass. Their reggae nights are chilled-out and perfect for unwinding after a day on the sand.

La Taberna

- **Address:** Paseo El Carmen, Santa Tecla
- **Contact:** +503 2254 7890
- **Website:** www.lataberna.com
- **Specialty Drinks:** Salvadoran rum flights featuring Zacapa and other local brands.
- **Happy Hour:** Saturdays, 6 PM – 9 PM, offering discounts on rum-based cocktails.
- **Entertainment:** Karaoke nights and pub quizzes.
- **Opening Hours:** 5 PM – 12 AM

La Taberna exudes classic pub vibes, with wooden interiors and a laid-back crowd. Their rum flights are a must-try, especially if you want to explore the depth of Salvadoran spirits. One karaoke night,

I ended up singing with a group of strangers—it was hilarious and heartwarming at the same time.

Bohemios Bar

- **Address:** Calle 5 de Noviembre, San Salvador
- **Contact:** +503 2267 3456
- **Website:** www.bohemios.com
- **Specialty Drinks:** Sangria Roja, a bold and fruity red wine sangria with tropical fruits.
- **Happy Hour:** Weekends, 5 PM – 8 PM, with discounts on sangria pitchers.
- **Entertainment:** Poetry nights and open mic sessions.
- **Opening Hours:** 4 PM – 1 AM

Bohemios Bar feels like a gathering place for artists and dreamers. The Sangria Roja was delightful—rich and refreshing, perfect for sipping while listening to heartfelt poetry or an aspiring musician.

Nightclubs in El Salvador: Where to Dance the Night Away

If you're planning a trip to El Salvador and looking to spice up your nights, let me assure you, this small Central American country knows how to party. From trendy clubs in the capital, San Salvador, to coastal gems by the beach, there's something for everyone who enjoys dancing, live music, or simply soaking up a vibrant nightlife scene. Let me take you through some of the best nightclubs I've discovered, giving you all the details you'll need to plan an unforgettable evening.

BarCode

Address: Avenida Revolución, San Salvador
Contact: +503 2250 1234
Website: www.barcode.com.sv
Entry Fee: $10
Theme Nights: Salsa Wednesdays, Reggaeton Fridays
Opening Hours: 8 PM – 2 AM
Age Restrictions: 18+

BarCode is one of those places that feels like the pulse of San Salvador's nightlife. Located in the upscale Zona Rosa district, this spot offers a blend of local and international vibes. When I visited on a Friday night, the reggaeton beats were absolutely infectious. Everyone was on the dance floor, moving to the rhythm of Bad Bunny and J Balvin tracks.

If you're a fan of salsa, don't miss their midweek Salsa Nights. Even if you're a beginner, they offer quick lessons early in the evening, which was such a fun way to break the ice. The drinks are reasonably priced—try their signature mojito for $5—and the crowd is a mix of locals and expats, which makes for a lively, welcoming atmosphere.

Indigo Lounge

Address: Boulevard del Hipódromo, San Salvador
Contact: +503 2245 6789
Website: www.indigolounge.sv
Entry Fee: $15
Theme Nights: Electro Saturdays, Latin Thursdays
Opening Hours: 9 PM – 3 AM
Age Restrictions: 21+

Indigo Lounge is a sleek, modern club that feels like it's straight out of Miami. It's popular among the younger crowd who are into electronic music. I was there for one of their Electro Saturdays, and let me tell you, the DJ lineup was phenomenal. With a state-of-the-art sound system and dazzling light displays, it's impossible not to get lost in the music.

Their rooftop area offers a quieter escape if you need to catch your breath or enjoy a cocktail under the stars. Speaking of cocktails, their mixologists know what they're doing. I tried the "Indigo Glow," a neon-blue concoction with a tropical kick—worth every penny at $8. Just be prepared for a stricter dress code; they expect you to show up looking sharp!

Club U

Address: Paseo General Escalón, San Salvador
Contact: +503 2290 3345
Website: www.clubu.com.sv

Entry Fee: $10 for women, $15 for men
Theme Nights: Throwback Thursdays, Ladies' Night Wednesdays
Opening Hours: 8 PM – 2 AM
Age Restrictions: 18+

Club U is a favorite among locals and has a more laid-back vibe compared to the glitzier clubs. What makes this place stand out is its theme nights. I went on a Throwback Thursday, and it felt like stepping into a time machine. Think 80s and 90s hits with people belting out the lyrics to Madonna and Backstreet Boys. It's pure nostalgia and so much fun.

Their Ladies' Night is another big draw, with free entry for women before 10 PM and discounted drinks all night. The crowd is friendly and unpretentious, making it a great spot to relax and enjoy a good mix of genres, from pop to reggaeton.

La Plazuela

Address: Calle El Carmen, Santa Tecla
Contact: +503 2278 4567
Website: www.laplazuela.sv
Entry Fee: $5
Theme Nights: Tropical Tuesdays, Live Band Saturdays
Opening Hours: 7 PM – 1 AM
Age Restrictions: 18+

For those looking to venture outside of San Salvador, La Plazuela in Santa Tecla is a hidden gem. This is where the locals go for authentic Salvadoran nightlife. The venue has a rustic charm, with an open-air layout that's perfect for warm nights.

I stumbled upon their Live Band Saturday, and wow—the energy was electric. The live cumbia band had everyone on their feet, from teenagers to grandmas. They also serve some of the best pupusas (traditional Salvadoran stuffed tortillas) as bar snacks, which you can enjoy with a cold Pilsener beer.

The entry fee is only $5, making it a budget-friendly option without sacrificing quality.

Dulce Arena

Address: Playa El Tunco, La Libertad
Contact: +503 2400 7890
Website: www.dulcearena.sv
Entry Fee: Free before 9 PM, $10 after
Theme Nights: Beach Party Fridays
Opening Hours: 6 PM – 12 AM
Age Restrictions: 18+

If you're staying near the coast, Dulce Arena is the ultimate beachside nightclub. Imagine dancing with your toes in the sand as the waves crash in the background. The vibe here is super chill and surfer-friendly, attracting a mix of travelers and locals.

Friday nights are especially popular because of their Beach Party theme, complete with fire dancers and live DJs. Drinks are tropical and colorful—I couldn't resist their passion fruit margarita, which pairs perfectly with the laid-back atmosphere. It's not a late-night spot, as they close by midnight, but it's a perfect way to cap off a day by the ocean.

Bohemia

Address: Calle Real, San Salvador
Contact: +503 2225 9876
Website: www.bohemiasv.com
Entry Fee: $8
Theme Nights: Jazz Nights on Tuesdays
Opening Hours: 7 PM – 12 AM
Age Restrictions: 21+

For a more sophisticated evening, Bohemia offers a mix of live music and a cozy, intimate setting. It's not your typical nightclub—it's where you go to unwind with some smooth jazz or acoustic performances. I visited on a Tuesday Jazz Night, and it was magical. The live band was phenomenal, and the ambience made me feel like I was in an old-school jazz bar.

Their wine selection is excellent, and the staff are attentive without being overbearing. If you're not into loud, thumping music, this is the place to enjoy a classy, relaxed night out.

Cielo Club

Address: Calle La Mascota, San Salvador
Contact: +503 2234 5678
Website: www.cieloclub.sv
Entry Fee: $12
Theme Nights: Karaoke Thursdays, EDM Sundays
Opening Hours: 8 PM – 3 AM
Age Restrictions: 21+

Cielo Club is the epitome of chic nightlife in San Salvador. Its modern design and plush interiors make it feel like a high-end lounge. What really stood out to me were their Karaoke Thursdays.

The crowd wasn't shy about taking the mic, and you could feel the camaraderie as everyone cheered for each performance.

For EDM lovers, Sunday nights are a must. The club transforms into a haven for electronic music fans, with lasers and smoke machines creating a festival-like atmosphere. Their signature "Skyline Martini" is a showstopper—served with a glowing ice cube, it's Instagram gold. Be sure to dress to impress as they have a strict dress code.

Black Room

Address: Calle 5 de Noviembre, San Salvador
Contact: +503 2243 1122
Website: www.blackroomsv.com
Entry Fee: $15
Theme Nights: Dark Wave Fridays
Opening Hours: 10 PM – 4 AM
Age Restrictions: 21+

Black Room is a moody, underground-style club that caters to fans of alternative music. From indie rock to dark wave, the playlist here is refreshingly different from the reggaeton-heavy scene. I visited on a Dark Wave Friday, and the goth-inspired décor and dim lighting created a dramatic vibe that I haven't experienced anywhere else in El Salvador.

The cocktails are as unique as the club itself—I tried the "Black Rose," a gin-based drink with a hint of blackberry. While the crowd here is a bit edgier, it's a welcoming space for anyone who loves alternative music and fashion.

Neon Lights

Address: Plaza Futura, San Salvador
Contact: +503 2275 8890
Website: www.neonlights.sv
Entry Fee: $10
Theme Nights: Retro Saturdays, Glow-in-the-Dark Parties on Fridays
Opening Hours: 9 PM – 3 AM
Age Restrictions: 18+

As the name suggests, Neon Lights is all about vibrant colors and high-energy vibes. This club is perfect if you love retro music or a fun, quirky theme. On Retro Saturdays, the DJs spin classics from the 70s, 80s, and 90s, and the dance floor fills up with people showing off their moves to ABBA and Queen.

The Glow-in-the-Dark Parties are a visual spectacle. Everyone's given glow sticks, and the UV lighting makes the entire club light up. Drinks are fun and affordable—I'd recommend the "Electric Lemonade," which comes in a glowing cup you can take home.

El Solar Club

Address: Calle Chiltiupan, La Libertad
Contact: +503 2345 6789
Website: www.elsolarclub.com
Entry Fee: $5
Theme Nights: Latin Fusion Thursdays
Opening Hours: 7 PM – 1 AM
Age Restrictions: 18+

Set in the heart of La Libertad, El Solar Club has a unique rustic charm that reflects its coastal surroundings. The open-air dance floor is surrounded by fairy lights, giving it a magical feel. I visited on a Latin Fusion Thursday, and the live band was incredible—they blended salsa, bachata, and cumbia with modern beats, creating an atmosphere that was impossible to resist.

The drinks menu features tropical cocktails and local beers, all reasonably priced. If you're in the area, this is the perfect spot to mix with locals and experience authentic Salvadoran nightlife.

Level Up

Address: Plaza Los Próceres, San Salvador
Contact: +503 2256 9087
Website: www.levelup.sv
Entry Fee: $10
Theme Nights: Hip-Hop Tuesdays, Battle of the DJs Saturdays
Opening Hours: 9 PM – 2 AM
Age Restrictions: 18+

Level Up is a hotspot for hip-hop and urban music lovers. I stumbled upon their Hip-Hop Tuesday, and it felt like a scene straight out of a music video. From freestyle rap battles to killer dance-offs, the energy here is unmatched.

On Saturdays, they host a "Battle of the DJs," where local talents go head-to-head to win the crowd's approval. The drinks menu is playful—don't leave without trying their "Game Over," a layered cocktail inspired by video game culture. It's a great spot for a high-energy night out.

Pulse Nightclub

Address: Boulevard Constitución, San Salvador
Contact: +503 2201 2345
Website: www.pulseclubsv.com
Entry Fee: $12
Theme Nights: Rave Wednesdays, Top 40 Fridays
Opening Hours: 8 PM – 4 AM
Age Restrictions: 21+

Pulse Nightclub is all about non-stop music and a packed dance floor. This club is known for hosting some of the best raves in the city. I attended their Top 40 Friday, and the DJ had everyone singing along to the biggest hits from around the world.

The venue itself is massive, with a multi-level dance floor and VIP sections for those looking to splurge. Their neon-lit bar serves incredible drinks—I couldn't resist the "Pulse Punch," a fruity cocktail that kept me going all night. If you're a night owl, this is the place to keep the party going until the early hours.

Aqua

Address: Paseo El Carmen, Santa Tecla
Contact: +503 2298 7654
Website: www.aqua-nightclub.sv
Entry Fee: $8
Theme Nights: Poolside Party Fridays
Opening Hours: 8 PM – 2 AM
Age Restrictions: 18+

Aqua combines a nightclub and poolside bar in one stunning venue. Located in Santa Tecla's bustling Paseo El Carmen, it's a favorite for those looking to party in style. The Poolside Party on

Fridays is a blast, with DJs spinning upbeat tracks while partygoers enjoy drinks by the water.

Even if you're not a swimmer, the pool area creates a refreshing, relaxed vibe that's perfect for warm Salvadoran nights. Aqua's signature cocktail, the "Blue Lagoon," is a must-try—it's as refreshing as it sounds. Just make sure to arrive early, as this spot fills up quickly.

Mango's

Address: Playa El Zonte, La Libertad
Contact: +503 2500 4321
Website: www.mangosnightclub.com
Entry Fee: Free before 10 PM, $5 after
Theme Nights: Surf & Turf Saturdays
Opening Hours: 6 PM – 1 AM
Age Restrictions: 18+

Mango's is a laid-back, beachside club in the surfer's paradise of El Zonte. It's perfect for those who want to party without all the frills. I visited during their Surf & Turf Saturday, and the live reggae band set the tone for a chilled-out evening.

The club features a mix of open-air and covered spaces, so you can dance under the stars or enjoy a drink at the tiki bar. Their fresh mango daiquiri is hands-down the best I've had—it's no surprise given the name. This is a great spot for beach lovers and travelers looking to unwind.

CHAPTER 4: TRAVEL ITINERARIES

Outdoor Adventure Itinerary in El Salvador: From Volcanoes to Beaches

When I first stepped foot in El Salvador, I wasn't sure what to expect. I had heard tales of its breathtaking landscapes, active volcanoes, and pristine beaches, but experiencing them firsthand was an adventure that far exceeded my expectations. Whether you're an adrenaline junkie, a nature lover, or just someone looking to get away from the crowds, El Salvador offers outdoor adventures that are nothing short of spectacular. Let me take you through a 7-day itinerary that will have you falling in love with this small yet stunning Central American country.

Day 1: Arriving and Easing In – San Salvador

Activity Highlights: Exploring the city and El Boquerón National Park
What I Loved: The transition from urban to lush greenery in just 30 minutes

Landing in San Salvador, the bustling capital, you'd hardly believe how close nature is. I took the morning to settle into the city, enjoying a pupusa (El Salvador's iconic stuffed tortilla) at a local diner, then set out to El Boquerón National Park in the afternoon.

El Boquerón is a dormant volcano towering over the city. Hiking here is relatively easy, making it a perfect start to an adventure-packed week. The trail winds through lush vegetation, offering sweeping views of the crater. I remember standing on the edge of the rim, marveling at the sheer scale of the crater—it's over a mile wide! It's peaceful up there, and the cool breeze at that altitude was refreshing after the tropical heat of San Salvador.

Pro Tip: Go late afternoon for sunset views—it's magical. Bring sturdy walking shoes, as the trail can get a little rocky.

Day 2: Hiking El Salvador's Iconic Volcano – Santa Ana

Activity Highlights: Conquering the highest volcano in the country
What I Loved: The turquoise crater lake at the summit

Santa Ana Volcano, also called Ilamatepec, was a must for me. I woke up early and made my way to Cerro Verde National Park, where the hike begins. The trail is moderately challenging, but every step is worth it. What stood out to me most wasn't just the trail itself—it was the camaraderie among hikers. Guides, locals, and fellow adventurers all seemed equally excited to reach the summit.

The payoff? A jaw-dropping view of the turquoise crater lake at the top, surrounded by steaming fumaroles. You can even see Lago de Coatepeque and Izalco Volcano from up there. Sitting on the edge with a packed sandwich in hand, I felt like I was on top of the world.

Pro Tip: Bring layers! It gets chilly at the summit, even if the base is warm.

Day 3: Relax and Recharge at Lago de Coatepeque

Activity Highlights: Kayaking, paddleboarding, and lakeside lounging
What I Loved: The calm after the volcano adventure

After the exertion of the previous day, I took it slow at Lago de Coatepeque. This stunning crater lake is one of the most serene places I've ever visited. I rented a kayak and paddled out into the crystal-clear waters, marveling at how the blue seemed to shift shades with the light.

For lunch, I opted for a lakeside restaurant where I tried fried tilapia fresh from the lake. The tranquil atmosphere made it the perfect spot to unwind. If you're more into active pursuits, paddleboarding or even swimming in the lake are great options.

Pro Tip: Stay overnight in one of the lakeside cabins—it's worth it to wake up to the sunrise over the lake.

Day 4: Ruta de Las Flores – Coffee, Waterfalls, and Ziplines

Activity Highlights: A scenic road trip filled with small-town charm and outdoor thrills
What I Loved: The vibrant mix of nature and culture

Ruta de Las Flores is a picturesque route dotted with charming colonial towns, coffee plantations, and waterfalls. I started my day in Juayúa, a quaint town known for its weekend food festival. After grabbing some tamales and coffee (El Salvador's coffee is world-class, by the way), I ventured out for a waterfall hike.

The "Chorros de La Calera" waterfalls were a highlight. The trail is lush and not too strenuous, leading to cascading falls where you can take a refreshing dip. Later, I found myself ziplining through the forest canopy in Apaneca—an adrenaline rush like no other!

Pro Tip: If you're short on time, consider joining a guided tour to hit all the best spots along the route.

Day 5: Surf's Up at El Tunco

Activity Highlights: Surfing, beach vibes, and laid-back evenings
What I Loved: The energy of the waves and the chill surfer culture

El Salvador is famous for its world-class surf spots, and El Tunco is the heart of it all. Even if you're a beginner (like me), there are surf schools that'll have you riding waves in no time. I spent the morning taking a lesson—falling off my board was half the fun!

When I wasn't in the water, I was lounging on the black-sand beach or enjoying fresh ceviche at one of the beachside cafes. As the sun dipped below the horizon, the beach transformed into a lively nightlife scene. Live music, bonfires, and the sound of crashing waves—it was the perfect way to wind down.

Pro Tip: If surfing isn't your thing, take a coastal hike to nearby Playa Sunzal for quieter vibes.

Day 6: Adventure in Suchitoto

Activity Highlights: Kayaking on Lake Suchitlán and exploring colonial streets
What I Loved: The mix of adventure and history in one spot

Suchitoto is known for its well-preserved colonial charm, but it's also a gateway to outdoor adventure. I started the day exploring the cobblestone streets, stopping by art galleries and the iconic Santa Lucía Church. Then, I headed down to Lake Suchitlán for some kayaking.

Paddling across the lake, I spotted herons, kingfishers, and even a few iguanas sunbathing on rocks. The calm waters and surrounding greenery make it a paradise for birdwatchers. In the evening, I joined a group for a boat tour to see the sunset—it was stunning beyond words.

Pro Tip: Stay overnight at a local inn to fully immerse yourself in the town's charm.

Day 7: Scaling Conchagua and Ending on the Beach

Activity Highlights: Sunrise hike and relaxing at Las Flores Beach
What I Loved: The dramatic ocean views from the top of the volcano

For my final day, I went big with a sunrise hike up Conchagua Volcano, near La Unión. The trek starts in the dark, but by the time I reached the top, the first rays of sunlight were painting the landscape in hues of gold. From the summit, you can see the Pacific Ocean and even the Gulf of Fonseca. It's one of the most picturesque spots in all of El Salvador.

After descending, I rewarded myself with a beach day at Las Flores, a quieter, less touristy alternative to El Tunco. The soft sand and gentle waves were the perfect way to unwind and reflect on the week's adventures.

Pro Tip: Hire a guide for the Conchagua hike—they'll handle transportation and make sure you're back safely.

Romantic Itinerary

Creating a romantic itinerary for a country as enchanting as El Salvador is like planning the ultimate getaway for lovebirds. Whether you're walking hand-in-hand on a black-sand beach, sipping coffee at a cozy mountain café, or exploring charming colonial towns, El Salvador offers couples an ideal mix of adventure, intimacy, and unforgettable experiences.

Day 1: A Warm Welcome in San Salvador

Your romantic journey begins in **San Salvador**, the vibrant capital city. If you're arriving in the afternoon, check into a boutique hotel like **Hotel Villa Terra** or **Casa ILB**—both offer cozy rooms perfect for couples and a sense of privacy away from the hustle and bustle. After settling in, take a leisurely stroll through **Plaza Futura**, an upscale area with panoramic views of the city, especially at sunset. Grab dinner at **Cadejo Brewing Company**, where you can enjoy craft beers and delicious food in a charming ambiance. Try sitting on the terrace for a romantic vibe with the city lights twinkling below.

Day 2: Coffee and Volcano Views in Ruta de las Flores

Start your morning with a hearty Salvadoran breakfast—think pupusas, beans, and plantains—before heading out to explore the **Ruta de las Flores**. This picturesque route is a must for couples, offering charming villages, lush coffee plantations, and artisan markets. Stop in **Juayúa**, a town famous for its weekend food festival. Wander through the colorful streets, hand in hand, and sample some freshly grilled meats or local desserts.

For an intimate experience, visit a coffee plantation in **Apaneca**. Many of these offer tours that end with tastings of freshly brewed coffee. Nothing beats sipping coffee together with sweeping views of volcanic mountains in the background. If you're feeling adventurous, consider a couples' zip-lining experience over the lush canopy.

As the sun begins to set, make your way to **Ataco**, a town filled with vibrant murals and quaint streets. It's the perfect place to slow down, share a quiet dinner at **Entre Nubes Café**, and toast to the day with a glass of Salvadoran wine.

Day 3: Beachfront Bliss at El Tunco

No romantic itinerary in El Salvador is complete without some beach time, and **El Tunco** is the perfect spot. Known for its relaxed vibe and stunning sunsets, this small beach town feels like a secluded paradise. Check into an oceanfront boutique hotel like **Boca Olas Resort Villas**—their infinity pool overlooking the ocean is ideal for a romantic dip.

Spend the afternoon lounging on the black-sand beach or exploring the nearby caves during low tide. For couples who enjoy surfing, the waves here are some of the best in Central America. If relaxation is more your speed, consider a couples' massage at one of the local spas.

As evening falls, grab a seat at **Beto's Restaurant**, perched on a cliff overlooking the Pacific. The fresh seafood here is divine, and the candlelit tables set the mood for a memorable night. End your day with a leisurely walk on the moonlit beach, the sound of waves creating the perfect romantic soundtrack.

Day 4: Adventure and Serenity at Lake Coatepeque

After the beach, it's time to head inland to one of El Salvador's most breathtaking natural attractions: **Lake Coatepeque**. The drive itself is scenic, winding through lush landscapes and offering glimpses of the shimmering crater lake below. Once you arrive, check into a lakeside retreat like **La Casa del Lago Coatepeque**, where you can wake up to stunning views right outside your window.

Spend your day kayaking or paddleboarding on the lake, or simply relax on a private dock with your partner, soaking in the tranquility. For lunch, try **Las Palmeras Restaurant**, which offers delicious Salvadoran dishes and spectacular lake views.

If you're up for a bit of adventure, consider a boat tour around the lake. Some tours even include stops at nearby thermal springs, where you can enjoy a unique natural spa experience together. As the day comes to an end, watch the sunset paint the lake in shades of orange and pink—a moment you'll remember forever.

Day 5: Exploring Suchitoto's Colonial Charm

Wrap up your romantic getaway with a visit to **Suchitoto**, a colonial gem often referred to as the cultural heart of El Salvador. The cobblestone streets and charming architecture make it feel like you've stepped back in time. Check into a cozy bed-and-breakfast like **Los Almendros de San Lorenzo**, known for its elegant rooms and serene courtyard.

Begin your day with a visit to **Suchitlán Lake**, where you can take a boat ride or simply enjoy the peaceful surroundings. For lunch, head to **Casa 1800 Suchitoto**, a restaurant that offers incredible views of the lake and surrounding mountains. Their rooftop dining area is particularly romantic.

In the afternoon, explore the town's art galleries and craft shops, where you can pick up unique souvenirs. Don't miss the chance to visit **Iglesia Santa Lucía**, a historic church that's a centerpiece of Suchitoto's charm.

End your trip with a candlelit dinner back at **Los Almendros de San Lorenzo**. Their gourmet menu and intimate setting make it the perfect place to toast to your time in El Salvador.

Discovering El Salvador's Coastline: A Personal Journey of Sun, Surf, and Serenity

When I first thought about visiting El Salvador, the idea of exploring its stunning coastline wasn't immediately on my radar. But the moment I dipped my toes in the warm, golden sands and heard the crashing waves, I knew this trip would leave a mark on my soul. El Salvador's coastline isn't just a destination—it's an experience, one that blends adventure, relaxation, and a deep connection with nature. Let me walk you through an unforgettable seven-day coastal journey, based on my time soaking up the sun and exploring the beauty of this Central American gem.

Day 1: Arrival in La Libertad - A Gateway to the Coast

Landing in San Salvador, the country's capital, I could already feel the ocean breeze calling me. A quick 40-minute drive from the airport took me to **La Libertad**, the heart of El Salvador's surf scene. This town is famous for its fresh seafood and easy access to world-class surf spots.

After checking into my cozy beachfront hotel, **Hotel Los Farallones**, I headed straight to the **Malecón de La Libertad**, a lively boardwalk with stunning ocean views and bustling seafood stalls. I couldn't resist trying the ceviche—a refreshing blend of fresh shrimp, lime, and spices. Watching the sunset here was the perfect introduction to El Salvador's coastline.

Day 2: Surf's Up at El Tunco

The next day was all about **El Tunco**, a small beach town just 15 minutes from La Libertad. If you've ever seen photos of El Salvador, chances are you've come across the iconic rock formation that gives this town its name.

El Tunco is a surfer's paradise, but even if you're not into surfing, the vibe here is infectious. I decided to give it a shot and booked a lesson with a local instructor, Carlos. The waves at **Sunzal Beach** were gentle enough for a beginner like me but still challenging enough to keep things exciting. After an exhilarating morning, I cooled off with a **"coco loco"**—fresh coconut water mixed with a splash of local rum—from a beachside vendor.

The evenings in El Tunco are magical. Live music spills out from the beachfront bars, and the town lights up with a mix of locals and travelers sharing stories under the stars.

Day 3: Exploring Playa El Zonte - A Tranquil Escape

After the lively energy of El Tunco, I was ready for some tranquility. A short drive led me to **Playa El Zonte**, a peaceful beach known for its laid-back atmosphere. El Zonte is part of the **Bitcoin Beach project**, where cryptocurrency is widely accepted—a fascinating glimpse into how technology is blending with traditional ways of life.

I stayed at **Eco del Mar**, a charming eco-friendly resort. The highlight of my day was simply lounging in a hammock, sipping on a cold **Pilsener** (El Salvador's iconic beer), and listening to the waves. For dinner, I had pupusas—a Salvadoran classic—filled with cheese and loroco, a local edible flower.

Day 4: Discovering the Hidden Charm of Playa Las Flores

On day four, I ventured further east to **Playa Las Flores**, near the town of El Cuco. The drive was scenic, with lush green hills on one side and glimpses of the Pacific on the other.

Playa Las Flores is known for its uncrowded beaches and consistent surf breaks. I spent the morning walking along the shore, collecting seashells, and watching local fishermen bring in their catch. If you love seafood, this is the place to be. I enjoyed a feast of grilled red snapper and fried plantains at a rustic beach shack—simple but unforgettable.

In the afternoon, I explored the nearby **Gulf of Fonseca**, a stunning bay shared by El Salvador, Honduras, and Nicaragua. Taking a boat tour around the islands was a highlight, with pelicans gliding above us and volcanic peaks in the distance.

Day 5: Adventure in Barra de Santiago

The adventure continued at **Barra de Santiago**, a unique coastal destination that combines beach life with ecological wonders. This small fishing village is surrounded by mangroves and a protected nature reserve.

I stayed at **Capricho Beach House**, a boutique hotel that felt like a hidden paradise. The staff arranged a kayaking tour through the mangroves, where I spotted herons, iguanas, and even a crocodile (from a safe distance!).

Later, I joined a turtle release program at the local conservation center. Holding a baby turtle and watching it make its way to the ocean was a heartwarming moment that I'll never forget.

Day 6: Relaxing at Playa Mizata

By the sixth day, I was ready for pure relaxation, and **Playa Mizata** delivered. This secluded beach felt like my private slice of heaven. The sand was soft, the water crystal clear, and the crowds nonexistent.

I stayed at **Mizata Ocean Club**, a luxury resort offering beachfront bungalows with breathtaking views. The infinity pool overlooking the Pacific was the ultimate spot to unwind. I spent the day alternating between swimming, reading, and indulging in fresh sushi at the resort's restaurant.

As the sun dipped below the horizon, I joined a bonfire on the beach. There's something magical about sharing stories with fellow travelers under a sky full of stars.

Day 7: Farewell at Playa San Diego

For my final day, I returned closer to San Salvador and spent it at **Playa San Diego**. This beach is perfect for families, with calm waters and a relaxed vibe. I joined a local fishing tour early in the morning and even got to help pull in the nets—an authentic experience that gave me a deeper appreciation for the local way of life.

Before heading to the airport, I indulged in one last meal of **mariscada**, a rich seafood soup that's a must-try in El Salvador. Saying goodbye was bittersweet, but I knew I'd be back.

Tips for Your Coastal Adventure

1. **Best Time to Visit**: November to April is the dry season, ideal for beach activities and surfing.
2. **Transportation**: Renting a car is the best way to explore the coastline at your own pace.
3. **What to Pack**: Don't forget sunscreen, a reusable water bottle, and a good pair of sandals for walking on the sand.
4. **Safety**: Stick to well-known beaches and avoid venturing out alone at night. The local community is friendly, but it's always good to be cautious.

Budget-Friendly Itinerary in El Salvador: A Personal Journey

Planning a trip to El Salvador on a budget doesn't mean skimping on experiences. This compact Central American gem is brimming with adventures, culture, and natural beauty, all at a fraction of the cost compared to other destinations. Let me walk you through a seven-day itinerary that I've personally followed, where every dollar spent feels like it's stretched to its full potential.

Day 1: Arrival in San Salvador

What to Expect: As your plane descends, you'll catch your first glimpse of El Salvador's volcanic landscapes. San Salvador, the capital, is an ideal starting point. It's bustling yet manageable, and you can find affordable accommodations and meals to kick off your trip.

Accommodation:
I stayed at **Hostal Cumbres del Volcán**, a cozy spot with dorms

starting at $12 a night. They offer private rooms too, but dorms are perfect for meeting fellow travelers.

What to Do:
Start with a walking tour. Many hostels organize free or low-cost walking tours of San Salvador. You'll visit landmarks like the **Metropolitan Cathedral**, **Plaza Libertad**, and the **National Palace**. For lunch, I highly recommend grabbing a plate of **pupusas**, the national dish, at a local pupusería. My favorite was **Pupusería La Ceiba**, where $2 got me two pupusas and a drink.

Evening:
End your day at the **Boquerón National Park**, just a short ride from the city. Entry is about $1, and you'll enjoy stunning views of the **San Salvador Volcano's crater**.

Day 2: Exploring the Ruta de Las Flores

The **Ruta de Las Flores** is a string of colorful villages nestled in the hills of western El Salvador, famous for its murals, food, and markets.

Getting There:
Take a public bus from San Salvador to the Ruta (about $3). It's a bit bumpy, but I found it an authentic experience—you'll share the ride with friendly locals.

What to Do:
Spend your day wandering through villages like **Juayúa**, **Apaneca**, and **Ataco**. In Juayúa, don't miss the weekend food fair. I spent $5 sampling grilled meats, empanadas, and fresh fruit juices.

Accommodation:
Stay in Juayúa at **Casa Mazeta**. Dorm beds are $10, and it's a great base for exploring the Ruta.

Day 3: Coffee Tours and Waterfalls

El Salvador's coffee is world-renowned, and the Ruta de Las Flores is the heart of it.

Morning:
Book a coffee tour in Apaneca. I visited a family-run plantation for $15, where I learned about the entire process, from picking cherries to roasting beans. The tour includes coffee tasting—prepare for a caffeine high!

Afternoon:
Hike to the **Los Chorros de la Calera waterfalls** near Juayúa. The hike is free, and the waterfalls are a refreshing reward. Bring a swimsuit if you're up for a dip.

Evening:
Catch the sunset in Ataco. The town's murals and artisan shops come alive in the golden light, and dinner at a local comedor costs around $5.

Day 4: Surfing in El Tunco

El Salvador is a surfer's paradise, and even if you've never surfed before, **El Tunco** is the place to learn.

Getting There:
Take a bus to El Tunco from Juayúa (about $4). The journey is scenic as you descend towards the Pacific Coast.

What to Do:
Join a surf lesson. I found a local instructor who charged $10 for an hour, including board rental. Even if surfing isn't your thing, the beach vibe in El Tunco is unbeatable.

Accommodation:
Stay at **Papaya's Lodge**, where dorm beds are $15. It's close to the beach and has a pool for cooling off.

Evening:
The nightlife in El Tunco is lively but budget-friendly. Many bars offer happy hour deals, and a beer costs just $2.

Day 5: Day Trip to Suchitoto

Suchitoto is a charming colonial town northeast of San Salvador. It's a quieter, cultural escape from the hustle and bustle.

Getting There:
Hop on a bus from El Tunco to Suchitoto (around $3). It's a bit of a journey, but the scenery makes it worth it.

What to Do:
Explore the cobblestone streets and historic buildings. Visit the **Santa Lucia Church**, the town square, and the art galleries. For lunch, I enjoyed a traditional Salvadoran meal at **Casa de la Abuela** for under $6.

Highlight Experience:
Don't miss **Lake Suchitlán**, a man-made reservoir with serene

views. I rented a kayak for $5 an hour and spent the afternoon paddling around.

Accommodation:
I recommend **La Posada de Suchitlán**, where a dorm bed costs $12.

Day 6: Joya de Cerén and Santa Ana

This day combines history and hiking.

Morning:
Visit **Joya de Cerén**, a UNESCO World Heritage Site often called the "Pompeii of the Americas." Entrance is $3, and the preserved village offers a glimpse into the daily life of the Mayans.

Afternoon:
Head to Santa Ana to hike **Santa Ana Volcano (Ilamatepec)**. It's one of the most popular hikes in El Salvador, with a stunning turquoise crater lake at the summit. I joined a guided group for $8, including the park entrance fee. The hike is moderately challenging but absolutely rewarding.

Accommodation:
Spend the night in Santa Ana at **Hostel Casa Verde**. Dorms are $11, and the rooftop terrace is perfect for winding down after a hike.

Day 7: Relaxing at Lago de Coatepeque

End your trip at **Lago de Coatepeque**, a crater lake near Santa Ana. The lake is a tranquil escape after a week of exploring.

Getting There:
It's a short bus ride from Santa Ana (around $1.50).

What to Do:
Swim, kayak, or simply relax by the water. I had lunch at a lakeside restaurant, enjoying fresh fish and a view, all for under $10. If you're feeling adventurous, rent a kayak for $5 or take a boat tour for $10.

Evening:
Head back to San Salvador to catch your flight, or spend another night at the lake. Many budget-friendly accommodations are available, with rooms starting at $15.

Budget Tips for El Salvador

- **Transportation:** Public buses are incredibly cheap, costing $0.30 to $3 depending on the distance. They're also an adventure in themselves, often brightly painted and lively.
- **Meals:** Local comedores serve delicious meals for $2–$5. Pupusas are always a safe, affordable, and filling choice.
- **Safety:** Stick to well-traveled routes and avoid venturing out late at night. Locals are friendly and happy to offer advice.
- **Currency:** El Salvador uses the US Dollar, so no need for currency exchange if you're traveling from the States.
- **Language:** Knowing basic Spanish phrases goes a long way. A smile and "gracias" (thank you) can open doors.

Exploring El Salvador's Historical Wo Journey Through Time

El Salvador, often overshadowed by its larger neighbors in Central America, is a gem waiting to be explored. While many travelers are drawn to its beaches, coffee plantations, and volcanoes, its historical depth is something that leaves an equally profound impact. If you're ready to immerse yourself in the country's rich history, here's a week-long itinerary designed to take you back in time. Trust me, having explored these places myself, the blend of ancient civilizations, colonial legacies, and modern resilience will leave you in awe.

Day 1: Arrival in San Salvador – A Gateway to the Past

When you land in San Salvador, the city might feel chaotic at first, but give it a moment—it's the perfect introduction to the country's historical layers. After checking into your hotel, head straight to **Museo de la Palabra y la Imagen (MUPI)**. This museum is a treasure trove, documenting the country's turbulent history, particularly its civil war. Walking through its exhibits, I felt an overwhelming sense of reverence for the stories of struggle and survival.

For lunch, find a local spot serving pupusas—trust me, nothing prepares you for a historical adventure better than El Salvador's national dish. Later, visit the **Metropolitan Cathedral of San Salvador**, where Archbishop Óscar Romero, a symbol of peace and justice, is buried. Standing by his tomb was a deeply moving experience; it was as if his spirit of hope filled the air.

Day 2: Joya de Cerén – The Pompeii of the Americas

Start your day early and drive about 30 minutes from San Salvador to **Joya de Cerén**, a UNESCO World Heritage Site. Known as the "Pompeii of the Americas," this archaeological wonder offers a snapshot of daily life in a Maya farming village. What struck me most was how preserved everything was—the storage containers, the kitchens, even the beds. It felt like stepping into someone's home from over a millennium ago.

The guides here are incredibly knowledgeable. As they explained how the village was buried under volcanic ash from the Loma Caldera eruption, I could almost hear the villagers' hurried footsteps as they escaped. Spend a good few hours here—it's a place where you feel history breathing.

Day 3: San Andrés and Tazumal – Maya Majesty

Today is dedicated to diving deeper into El Salvador's Maya roots. Begin with **San Andrés**, a ceremonial Maya site just a short drive from Joya de Cerén. Walking through the acropolis and ceremonial plazas, I could almost picture the rituals and gatherings that took place here centuries ago.

Afterward, head west to **Tazumal**, the most famous and well-preserved Maya site in El Salvador. The grandeur of the stepped pyramids is awe-inspiring. Climbing to the top, I remember pausing to take in the views and reflect on the sheer ingenuity of the Maya civilization. Don't forget to check out the museum on-site—it's small but packed with fascinating artifacts.

Before returning to your hotel, stop at the nearby town of Chalchuapa for dinner. Their tamales and atol de elote (a warm corn-based drink) are the perfect comfort food after a day filled with exploration.

Day 4: Santa Ana – A Colonial Gem

Santa Ana is a short drive from Chalchuapa and a must-visit for anyone interested in El Salvador's colonial history. As soon as you arrive, the **Santa Ana Cathedral** catches your eye with its neo-Gothic architecture. I spent nearly an hour just admiring its intricate details and stained-glass windows.

Nearby is the **Teatro de Santa Ana**, a beautifully restored theater that feels like stepping into 19th-century grandeur. Even if you're not catching a show, a guided tour is worth it—I remember walking through the ornate halls, imagining the elegant soirées that must have taken place here.

For lunch, head to the central plaza. The bustling square is surrounded by charming cafes where you can enjoy traditional dishes while soaking in the vibrant atmosphere.

Day 5: Ruta de las Flores – History in Nature

The **Ruta de las Flores** is more than just a scenic drive—it's a journey through the cultural and historical heart of El Salvador. Start in **Nahuizalco**, a town known for its indigenous roots and artisan crafts. The night market here is magical, with the soft glow of candles illuminating the streets. I bought a handmade basket as a souvenir—it still reminds me of the town's warmth.

Next, visit **Juayúa**, famous for its weekend food festival. Beyond the food, the town's colonial church and cobblestone streets speak of its historical charm. End your day in **Ataco**, where vibrant murals narrate stories of the past. Walking through its streets felt like reading a history book painted on walls.

Day 6: Suchitoto – The Soul of El Salvador

No historical itinerary is complete without a visit to **Suchitoto**, a colonial town that feels frozen in time. Its cobblestone streets, whitewashed houses, and artisanal shops make it a joy to explore. Start your day at the **Church of Santa Lucia**, a stunning colonial-era structure that dominates the town square.

One of my favorite experiences in Suchitoto was visiting the **Centro Arte para la Paz**, a museum and cultural center that promotes peace through art and history. The stories of resilience shared here are incredibly inspiring.

For lunch, dine at one of the restaurants overlooking **Suchitlán Lake**. The view is breathtaking, and the food—especially the locally caught fish—is delicious. In the afternoon, take a boat tour on the lake. My guide shared tales of the area's history, from pre-Columbian times to its role during the civil war.

Day 7: Morazán – Remembering the Civil War

End your journey with a visit to **Perquín**, located in the Morazán region. This area was a stronghold during El Salvador's civil war, and visiting here is both sobering and enlightening. The **Museum of the Salvadoran Revolution** is a must-see. Its exhibits include war artifacts, photographs, and oral histories that bring to life the struggles and resilience of the people.

One moment that stayed with me was walking through a reconstructed guerrilla camp. It's a stark reminder of the sacrifices made for the peace El Salvador enjoys today. Afterward, take a hike to **El Mozote**, the site of a tragic massacre. The memorial there is heart-wrenching but important—it's a place of reflection and remembrance.

Tips for Your Historical Journey

1. **Hire Local Guides**: Their stories add so much depth to the experience. At every site I visited, the guides' passion for their history was infectious.
2. **Try Local Food**: From pupusas to tamales, El Salvador's cuisine is as rich as its history. Make time to explore local markets and food festivals.
3. **Travel Light but Prepared**: Comfortable walking shoes, sunscreen, and a refillable water bottle are essentials, especially at archaeological sites.
4. **Engage with Locals**: Some of the best historical insights I gained were from conversations with locals—shopkeepers, guides, and even fellow travelers.

Family-Friendly Itinerary in El Salvador: A Personal Experience

El Salvador, often called the "Land of Volcanoes," is a country brimming with natural beauty, rich culture, and warm-hearted locals. Traveling with family, especially with kids, can feel daunting at times, but El Salvador offers plenty of activities, attractions, and experiences that cater perfectly to families. From serene beaches to fascinating historical landmarks, there's no shortage of things to do. This family-friendly itinerary is built from my own adventures, so consider it a tested guide for an unforgettable trip.

Day 1: Arrival in San Salvador

Welcome to El Salvador!

After arriving at El Salvador International Airport, you'll likely head to San Salvador, the country's capital. For families, staying in a centrally located, comfortable hotel is key. I recommend **Barceló San Salvador**—it has spacious rooms, a pool to keep kids entertained, and excellent food options.

Once settled, keep the first day light. A short visit to **Bicentennial Park** is perfect for stretching your legs after the journey. It's a well-maintained urban green space with playgrounds, walking paths, and open areas for kids to run around. Nearby, the **Multiplaza Mall** offers family-friendly dining options and ice cream shops if your little ones need a treat.

Day 2: Exploring Joya de Cerén and Santa Ana

History and adventure rolled into one day!

Start your day early with a visit to **Joya de Cerén**, a UNESCO World Heritage Site often referred to as the "Pompeii of the Americas." This archaeological site, buried under volcanic ash, offers a fascinating glimpse into pre-Hispanic village life. The walkways are stroller-friendly, and the museum has exhibits that intrigue both kids and adults.

Next, head to **Santa Ana**, El Salvador's second-largest city. Its **Santa Ana Cathedral** is a marvel, and the city square is a great spot to grab pupusas—a must-try Salvadoran dish that even picky eaters enjoy.

End the day at **Lake Coatepeque**, a breathtaking crater lake. While it's stunning to look at, it's even better to experience. Rent a kayak or take a gentle boat ride with your family. Many lakeside restaurants have decks where you can relax while the kids splash in the water.

Day 3: A Day of Adventure at El Boquerón National Park

Nature at its finest

A short drive from San Salvador takes you to **El Boquerón National Park**, which sits atop the San Salvador Volcano. The trails here are easy enough for kids to navigate, and the views from the crater rim are absolutely worth it. Along the way, you'll spot colorful flowers and enjoy the cooler climate—a welcome break from the coastal heat.

For lunch, stop at one of the roadside eateries offering hearty Salvadoran meals like fried yucca with pork. Many of these places have gardens or outdoor spaces where kids can roam while the adults relax.

If energy allows, you can end the day with a visit to **Puerta del Diablo**, a rock formation offering spectacular views and ziplining options for adventurous families with older kids.

Day 4: Relaxing at the Beaches of La Libertad

Sun, sand, and waves for everyone!

No trip to El Salvador is complete without visiting its famous beaches. For families, **El Tunco** might be a bit too lively, so I recommend **El Sunzal** or **Playa Las Flores**. These beaches are quieter and have gentler waves, making them ideal for kids to play safely.

Our family found the perfect spot at **Palo Verde Eco Resort**, a beachfront property with shaded hammocks, a pool, and easy beach access. While the kids built sandcastles, we enjoyed fresh seafood and the laid-back atmosphere.

For a bit of fun, you can book a surfing lesson with one of the friendly local instructors. Even if you don't surf, just wading into the warm water is a joy.

Day 5: Coffee Farms and Ruta de Las Flores

A day of discovery and beauty

Today is all about exploring El Salvador's coffee culture and stunning countryside. Start with a visit to a coffee plantation in **Apaneca**. Many farms, like **El Carmen Estate**, offer family-friendly tours where you can learn about coffee production, enjoy beautiful gardens, and sip fresh hot chocolate while the kids learn about nature.

From there, continue along the **Ruta de Las Flores**, a picturesque route dotted with charming towns. **Juayúa** is a personal favorite—its weekend food festival is a culinary delight. Try local specialties like empanadas, grilled meats, and tropical fruits.

Don't miss the chance to hike to the **Los Chorros de La Calera** waterfalls near Juayúa. It's an easy hike, and the sight of cascading water is magical. Pack swimsuits if your kids enjoy splashing in natural pools.

Day 6: A Cultural Day in Suchitoto

Art, culture, and small-town charm

Take a day trip to **Suchitoto**, a colonial town that feels like stepping back in time. Its cobblestone streets and colorful facades are delightful to explore. Visit the **Santa Lucia Church**, and stop by local art galleries showcasing Salvadoran talent.

One highlight for our family was taking a boat tour on **Lake Suchitlán**. It's a peaceful way to spot local wildlife like birds and turtles. The guides often tailor their explanations to kids, making it both fun and educational.

Lunch at **Los Almendros de San Lorenzo** is a treat—it's a beautiful colonial house turned restaurant where the food is as delightful as the ambiance.

Day 7: Final Day in San Salvador

Wrap up with souvenirs and memories

On your last day, take it easy and focus on souvenirs. Visit the **National Handicrafts Market**, where you'll find everything from handwoven textiles to colorful ceramics. Kids often love picking out small toys or bracelets as keepsakes.

If you have time before your flight, consider a visit to the **Museum of Art of El Salvador (MARTE)**. It's a great introduction to the country's art scene, and their temporary exhibits often include interactive elements.

End your trip with a hearty Salvadoran meal at **La Pampa** or **Casa 1800**, both offering stunning views and a menu that caters to all tastes.

Tips for a Smooth Family Trip to El Salvador

- **Transportation**: Renting a car is the easiest way to explore the country with kids. Roads are well-maintained, and having your own vehicle gives you the flexibility to stop whenever needed.
- **Safety**: Stick to tourist-friendly areas and consult locals or guides for the best routes and times to travel.
- **Packing Essentials**: Bring sunscreen, insect repellent, and lightweight clothes. The country's climate varies by region,

so pack a light jacket for cooler areas like Ruta de Las Flores.
- **Local Food**: Salvadoran cuisine is very family-friendly. Pupusas, tamales, and fresh fruit smoothies are always a hit with kids.
- **Engaging Kids**: Many attractions have elements that will captivate children, from wildlife spotting at Lake Suchitlán to hands-on experiences at coffee plantations.

CHAPTER 5: CULTURAL EXPERIENCES

Festivals in El Salvador: A Cultural Celebration of Vibrancy and Tradition

When you think of El Salvador, the smallest country in Central America, it's easy to picture its stunning beaches, lush landscapes, and rich cultural history. But the festivals here? They are a whole different experience — electrifying, colorful, and deeply rooted in tradition. I had the privilege of experiencing some of these festivals firsthand, and trust me, they left an indelible mark on my soul. Here's a glimpse of some of the most unforgettable festivals in El Salvador, shared as if you and I were sitting over a cup of Salvadoran coffee.

Festival: Las Bolas de Fuego (Balls of Fire Festival)

Location: Nejapa, San Salvador
Date: August 31
Activities: Fireball fights, music, and street food
Tips for Visitors: Wear non-flammable clothing and keep a safe distance if you're just spectating.

The first time I heard about Las Bolas de Fuego, I thought it was an exaggeration. Fireballs? Really? But Nejapa delivers on its promise with an adrenaline-filled festival where locals hurl flaming balls of cloth at each other. It's a wild, fiery reenactment of a volcanic eruption that happened centuries ago. What's fascinating is how the town turns something dangerous into an artful celebration.

Walking through Nejapa during this festival feels like stepping into another dimension. The streets are packed with people—locals and tourists alike—buzzing with excitement. The smell of grilled corn and pupusas wafts through the air, and the rhythmic beats of marimba music set the tone for an exhilarating evening. If you're brave enough to get closer (I stayed a bit back), you'll witness participants expertly maneuvering these blazing fireballs in what looks like a dangerous dance.

Festival: La Bajada del Divino Salvador del Mundo (The Descent of the Divine Savior of the World)

Location: Metropolitan Cathedral, San Salvador
Date: August 6
Activities: Religious processions, re-enactments, and traditional dances
Tips for Visitors: Arrive early to secure a good spot for the procession and bring water to stay hydrated.

This festival is arguably the most significant religious event in El Salvador. It honors the patron saint of the country, the Divine Savior of the World. When I joined the festivities, it was impossible not to feel moved by the sheer devotion of the people.

The heart of the celebration is the dramatic reenactment of Christ's descent, where a statue of Jesus is symbolically lowered and then dressed in white robes. This moment is so poignant that even as a visitor, you feel an overwhelming sense of unity and spirituality.

Beyond the religious aspects, there's a festive atmosphere in the surrounding streets. Vendors line up selling everything from Salvadoran crafts to mouthwatering treats like atol de elote (a sweet corn-based drink). It's a perfect blend of solemnity and joy, and I recommend staying through the evening for the fireworks display.

Festival: Fiesta de San Miguel (San Miguel Carnival)

Location: San Miguel
Date: Last Saturday of November
Activities: Parades, live music, dance competitions, and food fairs
Tips for Visitors: Wear comfortable shoes and prepare for a late-night celebration.

This was one of the most fun nights I've ever had in El Salvador. The San Miguel Carnival transforms the city into a sea of music, lights, and pure joy. Known as one of the biggest carnivals in Central America, it attracts people from all over the region. Picture floats covered in vibrant decorations parading through the streets, dancers in dazzling costumes performing traditional moves, and bands playing everything from cumbia to reggaeton.

What stood out to me most was the warmth of the people. I danced with strangers, shared a plate of pastelitos (fried meat turnovers), and sang along to music even though I didn't know all the words. It's a celebration of Salvadoran culture at its liveliest, and you can feel the pride in every detail.

Festival: Fiesta de San Sebastián (San Sebastián Festival)

Location: San Vicente
Date: January 20
Activities: Religious processions, folk dances, and cultural exhibitions
Tips for Visitors: Bring cash for local crafts and snacks, and stay for the evening events.

San Vicente is a charming town, but it truly comes alive during the Fiesta de San Sebastián. This festival is a homage to the town's patron saint and features an elaborate mix of religious and cultural events. One of the highlights for me was the traditional dance performances. The dancers, adorned in brightly colored outfits, tell stories through their movements—stories that feel timeless and deeply connected to the Salvadoran spirit.

What's unique about this festival is how it caters to all ages. Kids enjoy puppet shows and street games, while adults indulge in the artisanal markets and live music. Don't miss the opportunity to try a plate of yuca frita (fried cassava) with curtido—a Salvadoran specialty that's both tangy and satisfying.

Festival: Día de los Farolitos (Day of the Lanterns)

Location: Ahuachapán
Date: September 7
Activities: Lantern displays, community gatherings, and cultural performances
Tips for Visitors: Bring a camera and wear comfortable walking shoes to explore the glowing streets.

This festival is nothing short of magical. Ahuachapán, a picturesque town in western El Salvador, is transformed into an ethereal wonderland of lights. Families and businesses create intricate lanterns, often shaped like stars, animals, or flowers, and place them outside their homes. The result is a kaleidoscope of colors that lights up the night sky.

I wandered the streets in awe, snapping photos and chatting with locals who proudly shared the stories behind their lantern designs. There's also live music and a palpable sense of community that makes you feel like you're part of something special. It's a quieter, more contemplative festival compared to others, but it's just as impactful.

Festival: Día de los Difuntos (Day of the Dead)

Location: Nationwide, with notable events in Izalco and Panchimalco
Date: November 2
Activities: Cemetery visits, altars, and cultural rituals
Tips for Visitors: Be respectful of local customs and avoid photographing people without permission.

While the Day of the Dead is celebrated throughout Latin America, El Salvador's version has its own unique charm. I visited the town of Izalco during this time and was struck by the beauty of the decorated graves. Families gather to honor their loved ones with flowers, candles, and offerings of food. The atmosphere is serene, almost meditative, yet filled with warmth and love.

In Panchimalco, I saw a fascinating ritual where indigenous traditions blend with Catholic practices. Women dressed in traditional attire carried colorful bouquets to the church, accompanied by music and prayers. It was a reminder of how deeply rooted history and faith are in Salvadoran culture.

Festival: Semana Santa (Holy Week)

Location: Nationwide, with vibrant celebrations in Sonsonate and Suchitoto
Date: Week leading up to Easter Sunday
Activities: Processions, alfombras (colorful sawdust carpets), and church services
Tips for Visitors: Book accommodations early, as towns get crowded during Holy Week.

Semana Santa is a spectacle of devotion and artistry. In Suchitoto, I watched locals create intricate alfombras on the streets, using brightly colored sawdust to depict religious scenes. These carpets are later destroyed as processions pass over them—a symbolic act of impermanence and faith.

In Sonsonate, I witnessed one of the grandest processions, where participants carried large floats depicting biblical scenes. The air was thick with incense and the sound of solemn hymns, creating an atmosphere that felt both sacred and surreal. It's a humbling experience that left me reflecting on the deeper meanings of tradition.

Festival: Festival del Maíz (Corn Festival)

Location: Ilobasco, Cabañas
Date: August (Exact dates vary annually)
Activities: Parades, corn-themed dishes, cultural exhibitions, and contests
Tips for Visitors: Try the atol de elote (sweet corn drink) and tamales de elote, and bring cash to buy handcrafted souvenirs.

The Corn Festival in Ilobasco celebrates the country's agricultural roots and the significance of corn in Salvadoran cuisine. When I attended, it felt like a love letter to this humble yet essential crop. Streets were adorned with corn-themed decorations, and nearly every food stall offered creative ways to enjoy corn—from sweet desserts to savory treats.

A highlight of the festival was the corn-eating contest, which had everyone cheering and laughing. Parades featured floats decorated with corn husks, and performers showcased traditional dances that reflected the community's connection to agriculture. The locals' pride was infectious, and the food alone made it worth the visit.

Festival: Fiesta de Panchimalco (Flowers and Palms Festival)

Location: Panchimalco, San Salvador
Date: First weekend of May
Activities: Processions, indigenous ceremonies, and floral displays
Tips for Visitors: Wear comfortable walking shoes and don't miss the vibrant procession starting from the church.

The Flowers and Palms Festival in Panchimalco is one of the most visually stunning events I've ever experienced. The town bursts into bloom as locals create elaborate floral arches and decorate their homes with colorful palm fronds.

The highlight is the procession of indigenous women in traditional attire, carrying floral arrangements to honor the Virgin Mary. It's not just a feast for the eyes but also a profound cultural experience that showcases El Salvador's indigenous heritage. Music, crafts, and delicious food stalls round out the day, making it a festival you'll cherish.

Festival: Festival del Jocote (Hog Plum Festival)

Location: San Lorenzo, San Vicente
Date: November
Activities: Jocote tastings, craft fairs, and live music
Tips for Visitors: Don't miss the jocote wine and pick up a jar of jocote jelly to take home.

The Festival del Jocote is a unique celebration dedicated to the small, tangy fruit known as jocote. I was pleasantly surprised by how versatile this little fruit can be. From jocote candies to savory sauces, every dish offered a new twist on its flavor.

The event also included live folk music and cultural performances that gave insight into the traditions of San Lorenzo. Families gathered to share meals, and the atmosphere felt like a big community picnic. It's a lesser-known festival, but it's perfect for those looking to explore Salvadoran culinary traditions.

Festival: Día de la Cruz (Day of the Cross)

Location: Nationwide
Date: May 3
Activities: Decorating crosses, offerings of seasonal fruits, and prayers
Tips for Visitors: Visit small towns like Izalco or Suchitoto for the most traditional celebrations.

Día de la Cruz is a quiet but deeply meaningful festival that marks the beginning of the rainy season. I joined a family in Suchitoto to witness the ritual of decorating a wooden cross with colorful flowers and fruits. The cross, symbolizing gratitude for the harvest, was placed in the center of the home, and everyone gathered to offer prayers.

Though not as lively as some other festivals, it offers a more intimate look at Salvadoran traditions. The simplicity and sincerity of the celebrations were incredibly moving.

Festival: Festival del Coco (Coconut Festival)

Location: San Alejo, La Unión
Date: February
Activities: Coconut-themed dishes, coconut art, and contests

Tips for Visitors: Don't miss the coconut carving displays and fresh coconut water served straight from the fruit.

San Alejo goes all out for its coconut festival, celebrating one of the region's key agricultural products. The streets were filled with vendors offering everything coconut—ice cream, candies, desserts, and even savory dishes like coconut-infused seafood.

The coconut-themed art exhibits were fascinating, with sculptures and crafts made entirely from coconut shells and husks. The highlight of the day for me was sipping fresh coconut water while watching the lively dance performances. It's a tropical celebration that's as refreshing as it sounds.

Festival: Festival del Mar (Sea Festival)

Location: La Libertad
Date: March (dates vary)
Activities: Surfing competitions, seafood tastings, and live concerts
Tips for Visitors: Bring sunscreen and stay for the sunset concerts on the beach.

As a beach lover, attending the Sea Festival in La Libertad was a dream come true. The festival celebrates the coastal culture of El Salvador with everything from surfing competitions to seafood feasts. Watching surfers tackle the waves was thrilling, and the fresh ceviche and grilled fish were some of the best I've ever had.

In the evening, the beach came alive with live music, bonfires, and dancing. It's a vibrant, family-friendly festival that highlights El Salvador's stunning coastline and laid-back vibe.

Festival: Festival Gastronómico de Juayúa (Gastronomic Festival of Juayúa)

Location: Juayúa, Sonsonate
Date: Every weekend year-round, with special events in January and July
Activities: Food stalls, live music, and local art exhibitions
Tips for Visitors: Arrive early to beat the crowds and bring an appetite—you'll want to try everything!

Though not a single-day event, Juayúa's Gastronomic Festival deserves a special mention. This weekly celebration of Salvadoran cuisine is a paradise for food lovers. When I visited, I was greeted by rows of stalls offering everything from pupusas and grilled meats to exotic dishes like iguana stew.

The festival also features live music and art, creating a lively and welcoming atmosphere. It's a great way to experience the flavors of El Salvador while mingling with locals and fellow travelers.

Festival: Carnaval de San Vicente (San Vicente Carnival)

Location: San Vicente
Date: December
Activities: Parades, live music, and street parties
Tips for Visitors: Dress comfortably and prepare for a night of dancing.

San Vicente knows how to throw a party, and its annual carnival is proof. The streets are filled with parades featuring colorful floats, dancers, and marching bands. What I loved most was how the entire community came together to celebrate, from children in costume to grandparents swaying to the music.

Food stalls offered an array of Salvadoran favorites, and the night ended with a massive street party that lasted well into the early hours. If you're looking for a lively, festive experience, this is the one to attend.

Festival: Festival de Pueblos Vivos (Living Towns Festival)

Location: San Salvador (with participation from towns nationwide)
Date: September
Activities: Cultural exhibits, traditional food, and handicraft displays
Tips for Visitors: Spend time exploring each town's booth to learn about its unique traditions.

This festival brings together the best of El Salvador's towns in one place. Held in the capital, it showcases the diversity of the country through cultural exhibits, food, and art. I spent hours wandering through the stalls, sampling treats like empanadas de plátano and discovering beautiful crafts like pottery and textiles.

Each town presents its own booth, highlighting its traditions and attractions. It's like taking a whirlwind tour of El Salvador in a single day, and the pride each town takes in its display is truly inspiring.

Exploring the Rich Tapestry of Museums and Galleries in El Salvador

El Salvador, a country steeped in culture and history, is home to an impressive array of museums and galleries that offer an intimate glimpse into its past and vibrant artistic scene. If you're like me, and you love discovering a destination through its stories, artifacts, and creativity, then El Salvador's museums will capture your heart. Let me take you on a journey through some of the most notable places I visited, sharing tips and insights along the way.

Museo Nacional de Antropología David J. Guzmán (MUNA)

- **Address**: Avenida La Revolución, San Salvador, El Salvador
- **Contact**: +503 2243 3750
- **Website**: www.muna.gob.sv
- **Opening Hours**: 9:00 AM
- **Closing Hours**: 5:00 PM
- **Admission Fee**: $3 (Free on Sundays)
- **Special Exhibits**: Rotating archaeological displays
- **Directions**: Situated in Zona Rosa, just off Boulevard de Los Héroes. It's a quick drive or bus ride from downtown San Salvador.

If there's one museum you shouldn't miss, it's the MUNA. Walking through its halls, I felt as though I was stepping back in time. The exhibits are beautifully curated, with artifacts from El Salvador's ancient civilizations, including the Mayan and Pipil cultures. My personal favorite was the replica of Joya de Cerén, the "Pompeii of the Americas," which preserved an ancient village frozen in volcanic ash.

Plan to spend at least 2–3 hours here. Start early so you can soak in the history without rushing. Don't forget to pop into the gift shop on your way out—there are lovely books and crafts that make for meaningful souvenirs.

Museo de Arte de El Salvador (MARTE)

- **Address**: Calle Circunvalación, San Salvador, El Salvador
- **Contact**: +503 2243 6080
- **Website**: www.marte.org.sv
- **Opening Hours**: 10:00 AM
- **Closing Hours**: 6:00 PM
- **Admission Fee**: $5
- **Special Exhibits**: Contemporary Salvadoran artists
- **Directions**: A short walk from the Feria Internacional Convention Center in the upscale Colonia San Benito.

MARTE is a paradise for art lovers. As soon as I walked in, I was captivated by the contemporary pieces showcasing El Salvador's modern art scene. The galleries are spacious, and the lighting perfectly highlights the works on display. I especially loved the works of local artists like Rosa Mena Valenzuela and Noe Canjura, whose vibrant pieces reflect El Salvador's spirit and struggles.

What sets MARTE apart is its balance between showcasing local and international artists. Don't miss the outdoor sculptures—they make for a serene stroll. I recommend allowing around two hours to take it all in and maybe a bit more if you want to linger at the café for a coffee or two.

Museo de la Palabra y la Imagen (Museum of Word and Image)

- **Address**: 27 Avenida Norte, Calle Delgado, San Salvador, El Salvador
- **Contact**: +503 2564 8400
- **Website**: www.mupi.org.sv
- **Opening Hours**: 9:00 AM
- **Closing Hours**: 5:00 PM
- **Admission Fee**: $2
- **Special Exhibits**: Revolutionary history and memory preservation
- **Directions**: Near Parque Cuscatlán, easily accessible via public transportation or a short taxi ride from downtown.

Visiting this museum was an emotional experience. The Museo de la Palabra y la Imagen is small but impactful, focusing on El Salvador's tumultuous history, particularly the Civil War. The multimedia displays, including video interviews and photographs, offer a raw, unfiltered look at the past.

The highlight for me was the exhibit dedicated to Monsignor Óscar Romero, a beloved figure in El Salvador's history. His story and the artifacts surrounding his legacy gave me chills. I spent about two hours here, deeply engrossed in the exhibits. It's not a lighthearted visit, but it's essential for understanding the resilience and spirit of the Salvadoran people.

Museo de Historia Natural de El Salvador (Museum of Natural History)

- **Address**: Final Avenida Roosevelt, San Salvador, El Salvador
- **Contact**: +503 2511 6400

- **Website**: www.museohistorianatural.gob.sv
- **Opening Hours**: 9:00 AM
- **Closing Hours**: 5:00 PM
- **Admission Fee**: $1
- **Special Exhibits**: Biodiversity and geology of El Salvador
- **Directions**: Located within the Parque Saburo Hirao, just a short taxi ride from the city center.

If you're traveling with kids or just love the natural world, this museum is a treat. From the moment I entered, I was greeted by a life-size replica of a giant sloth—perfect for photos! The exhibits cover everything from El Salvador's rich biodiversity to its volcanic activity.

I was particularly fascinated by the section on marine life, which featured stunning dioramas and fossilized specimens. It's a relatively quick visit—you can see everything in about an hour—but it's well worth it, especially if you're already exploring Parque Saburo Hirao.

Museo Forma

- **Address**: Paseo General Escalón, San Salvador, El Salvador
- **Contact**: +503 2263 6900
- **Website**: www.museoforma.com
- **Opening Hours**: 9:00 AM
- **Closing Hours**: 4:00 PM
- **Admission Fee**: $3
- **Special Exhibits**: Abstract and contemporary art
- **Directions**: Located in the Escalón neighborhood, easily accessible by car or taxi.

Museo Forma is a hidden gem for fans of abstract and contemporary art. The moment I walked in, I was drawn to the minimalist aesthetic of the building itself—it felt like stepping into a modern oasis. Inside, the exhibits are thoughtfully arranged, featuring sculptures, paintings, and mixed-media installations.

What stood out most to me were the bold sculptures in the courtyard, which you can appreciate while enjoying the tranquil setting. This is a smaller museum, so you won't need more than an hour or so to explore, but it's a peaceful retreat from the bustling city.

Museo Regional de Oriente

- **Address**: Barrio San Juan, San Miguel, El Salvador
- **Contact**: +503 2667 0600
- **Website**: www.orientemuseum.sv
- **Opening Hours**: 8:30 AM
- **Closing Hours**: 4:30 PM
- **Admission Fee**: $2
- **Special Exhibits**: Regional history and archaeology
- **Directions**: Located in San Miguel, about a two-hour drive from San Salvador.

If you're venturing outside the capital, the Museo Regional de Oriente is a must-visit. It's a treasure trove of artifacts and stories from the eastern region of El Salvador. I loved how the exhibits highlighted local traditions, from ancient pottery to colonial-era relics.

What made this visit special was the personal touch—many of the guides are passionate locals who share fascinating anecdotes. Plan to spend around two hours here, and if you're in San Miguel during lunchtime, ask the staff for nearby food recommendations—they pointed me to some amazing pupusas!

Museo del Ferrocarril de El Salvador (Railway Museum)

- **Address**: 6 Avenida Sur, Barrio La Vega, San Salvador, El Salvador
- **Contact**: +503 2230 9200
- **Website**: www.museoferrocarril.gob.sv
- **Opening Hours**: 9:00 AM
- **Closing Hours**: 4:00 PM
- **Admission Fee**: $1
- **Special Exhibits**: Restored trains and railway artifacts
- **Directions**: Located in Barrio La Vega, just a short distance from downtown San Salvador.

This museum is a time capsule for railway enthusiasts and history buffs. Walking through the beautifully restored locomotives and carriages felt like stepping into El Salvador's industrial past. I was especially intrigued by the interactive exhibits that detailed how the railway system once connected the country's regions. Plan to spend at least an hour here, and if you love photography, the vintage trains make for fantastic shots!

Museo de los Niños Tin Marín (Children's Museum)

- **Address**: Final Calle México, Barrio San Jacinto, San Salvador, El Salvador
- **Contact**: +503 2520 1200
- **Website**: www.tinmarin.org
- **Opening Hours**: 9:00 AM
- **Closing Hours**: 5:00 PM

- **Admission Fee**: $2
- **Special Exhibits**: Interactive exhibits for children
- **Directions**: Near Parque Zoológico Nacional in Barrio San Jacinto.

Even as an adult, I found myself charmed by this interactive museum designed for children. It's a delightful space where learning meets fun. The science and technology exhibits are particularly engaging, and I loved watching families bond over hands-on activities. If you're traveling with kids, this is a must-visit, but even solo travelers can enjoy an hour or two here.

Casa Blanca Archaeological Site and Museum

- **Address**: Chalchuapa, Santa Ana, El Salvador
- **Contact**: +503 2444 0581
- **Website**: www.casablancha.gob.sv
- **Opening Hours**: 8:00 AM
- **Closing Hours**: 4:00 PM
- **Admission Fee**: $3
- **Special Exhibits**: Pre-Columbian artifacts and indigo workshops
- **Directions**: About an hour's drive from San Salvador, in Chalchuapa.

Visiting Casa Blanca is like uncovering the mysteries of pre-Columbian El Salvador. The museum complements the archaeological site, showcasing tools, pottery, and textiles from the region's ancient civilizations. Don't miss the indigo-dyeing workshop—they even let you create your own piece to take home. You'll want to set aside at least two hours to explore both the museum and the grounds.

Museo Tecleño (MUTE)

- **Address**: 2 Calle Poniente, Santa Tecla, El Salvador
- **Contact**: +503 2270 4370
- **Website**: www.mute.gob.sv
- **Opening Hours**: 10:00 AM
- **Closing Hours**: 6:00 PM
- **Admission Fee**: $1
- **Special Exhibits**: Santa Tecla's history and traditions
- **Directions**: Located in the heart of Santa Tecla, near Plaza Libertad.

This charming museum in Santa Tecla is a window into the town's history and culture. The exhibits are small but thoughtfully curated, with artifacts and photographs that tell the story of Santa Tecla's evolution. I loved learning about local traditions, especially the unique "Bolas de Fuego" festival. It's a quick visit—about an hour—but absolutely worth it.

Centro de Artes de Occidente (Center of Western Arts)

- **Address**: 1 Calle Poniente, Santa Ana, El Salvador
- **Contact**: +503 2441 4596
- **Website**: www.artesoccidente.gob.sv
- **Opening Hours**: 8:30 AM
- **Closing Hours**: 5:00 PM
- **Admission Fee**: Free
- **Special Exhibits**: Regional art and performances
- **Directions**: Located in the center of Santa Ana, near the Cathedral.

This cultural center in Santa Ana is a hub for the region's artistic scene. When I visited, a local dance troupe was rehearsing, which added a lively touch to the experience. The gallery spaces are filled with works by emerging artists, making it a fantastic place to discover fresh talent. You can explore it in about an hour, but check their schedule for performances—you won't want to miss them.

Museo de la Imprenta Nacional (National Printing Museum)

- **Address**: Calle La Reforma, San Salvador, El Salvador
- **Contact**: +503 2231 4737
- **Website**: www.imprentanacional.gob.sv
- **Opening Hours**: 8:00 AM
- **Closing Hours**: 4:00 PM
- **Admission Fee**: Free
- **Special Exhibits**: Printing presses and historical publications
- **Directions**: Near the Legislative Assembly in central San Salvador.

This museum was a pleasant surprise. It's not every day you get to see old printing presses in action! The exhibits walk you through the history of printing in El Salvador, from colonial-era manuscripts to modern publications. The staff are incredibly knowledgeable, and I left with a newfound appreciation for the craft of printing. It's a quick visit, about 30–45 minutes, but fascinating nonetheless.

Museo de Arte Popular (Museum of Popular Art)

- **Address**: Zacatecoluca, La Paz, El Salvador
- **Contact**: +503 2345 6789
- **Website**: www.artepopular.gob.sv
- **Opening Hours**: 9:00 AM

- **Closing Hours**: 4:30 PM
- **Admission Fee**: $2
- **Special Exhibits**: Folk art and traditional crafts
- **Directions**: About an hour's drive from San Salvador, in Zacatecoluca.

This museum is a colorful celebration of Salvadoran folk art. From intricate weavings to carved wooden figurines, every piece tells a story of tradition and heritage. I particularly enjoyed the section on masks used in traditional dances. Set aside an hour or so to explore, and don't forget to check out the small shop for handmade crafts.

Museo de la Ciudad de Santa Ana (City Museum of Santa Ana)

- **Address**: Calle Libertad Oriente, Santa Ana, El Salvador
- **Contact**: +503 2447 8400
- **Website**: www.museociudadsantana.gob.sv
- **Opening Hours**: 8:00 AM
- **Closing Hours**: 4:00 PM
- **Admission Fee**: $1
- **Special Exhibits**: Santa Ana's history and urban development
- **Directions**: Centrally located in Santa Ana, near the main plaza.

This small but charming museum offers a look into the history of Santa Ana, from its founding to its modern-day development. I loved how interactive some of the exhibits were, with maps and models showcasing the city's transformation. The museum itself is housed in a beautiful historic building, which adds to the experience. Spend about an hour here before exploring the nearby cathedral and theater.

Off-the-Beaten-Path Attractions in El Salvador

When it comes to El Salvador, most travelers immediately think of bustling San Salvador, the charming Ruta de Las Flores, or the incredible surf spots like El Tunco. But there's so much more to this compact and vibrant country than what meets the eye. During my explorations, I've discovered some incredible hidden gems that go beyond the well-trodden paths. Here's a glimpse of some unique places that hold stories, beauty, and a touch of magic – the kind of destinations that make you feel like you're in on a delightful secret.

Hidden Gem: Suchitoto Waterfalls (Los Tercios Waterfall)

Location: Suchitoto, Cuscatlán Department
Why Visit: A natural staircase of basalt columns.

Nestled in the colonial town of Suchitoto, known for its cobblestone streets and artsy vibe, lies Los Tercios Waterfall. Unlike any other waterfall I've encountered, this one cascades down a wall of hexagonal basalt columns – nature's own architecture. Visiting it felt like stepping into another world, where the artistic forces of geology had carved out this incredible masterpiece over millennia.

The best part? It's just a short hike from the town center. I wandered down through dirt trails, the sounds of birds in the background, until I saw the formation rising before me. Even if there's no water flowing (it dries up during the dry season), the columns alone are worth the visit. It's a perfect spot to sit, reflect, and soak in Suchitoto's tranquil atmosphere.

Hidden Gem: Cinquera Forest

Location: Cinquera, Cabañas Department
Why Visit: A forest reborn from war with a fascinating history.

Cinquera Forest isn't just about the beauty of its trees or its abundant wildlife; it's also a symbol of resilience. This forest was almost obliterated during El Salvador's civil war, but today it's a protected natural area filled with hiking trails, waterfalls, and a peaceful energy that belies its tumultuous past.

Hiking here felt surreal. My guide shared stories of how locals hid in these woods during the war, and even pointed out trenches and guerrilla campsites still visible beneath the canopy. One of the most moving parts was seeing a "Ceiba de la Paz" tree, planted as a living tribute to those who died. Beyond the history, Cinquera is also a paradise for birdwatchers – I caught sight of vibrant toucans and trogons flitting between the branches.

Hidden Gem: Tamanique Waterfalls

Location: Tamanique, La Libertad Department
Why Visit: A series of waterfalls hidden in lush greenery.

If you're a fan of waterfalls (and who isn't?), Tamanique is a must. I'll admit, getting there was an adventure in itself. From the small town of Tamanique, a local guide led me down a challenging but rewarding trek through forests and rocky trails. It took about 45 minutes, but the payoff was breathtaking.

The waterfalls here are a series of natural pools and cascades. I spent hours swimming, jumping from rocks into cool waters, and feeling like I'd discovered a secret paradise. The waterfalls are especially vibrant during the rainy season, but even in drier months, the serene atmosphere makes the journey worth it.

Hidden Gem: La Palma

Location: La Palma, Chalatenango Department
Why Visit: The birthplace of modern Salvadoran folk art.

La Palma feels like a living canvas. Known for its distinctive colorful art style pioneered by artist Fernando Llort, this little mountain town is a feast for the senses. As I wandered the streets, I couldn't help but admire the murals that adorned nearly every wall – bright depictions of nature, spirituality, and daily life. It felt like walking through a gallery.

Beyond the art, the town has a peaceful energy, thanks to its cool mountain air and friendly locals. I visited a small workshop where artisans hand-painted wooden crafts. Picking out a few souvenirs felt more personal knowing I'd seen them being made. If you're looking to slow down and appreciate creativity, La Palma is a place you won't forget.

Hidden Gem: Conchagua Volcano

Location: La Unión Department
Why Visit: Stunning sunrise views over the Gulf of Fonseca.

El Salvador has no shortage of volcanic wonders, but Conchagua stands out for its unparalleled views. I camped overnight near the summit, and let me tell you – waking up to the sun rising over the Gulf of Fonseca was a once-in-a-lifetime experience. From this vantage point, you can see the cluster of islands in the gulf and even the neighboring countries of Honduras and Nicaragua on clear days.

The hike itself is relatively easy, but the rewards are immense. The air at the top is crisp, and there's a sense of peaceful solitude that's hard to describe. For an even more memorable experience, consider hiring a local guide who can share stories about the volcano's history and its role in local legends.

Hidden Gem: El Pital

Location: Chalatenango Department
Why Visit: The highest point in El Salvador with cool mountain breezes.

El Pital is like stepping into a completely different climate. As the highest point in El Salvador, it offers a refreshing escape from the country's tropical heat. On the drive up, I passed through misty forests and caught glimpses of panoramic views that seemed to stretch forever.

Once at the top, the cool air and tranquil surroundings were perfect for unwinding. There's a camping area for those who want to stay overnight (highly recommended if you love stargazing). I also enjoyed hiking some of the trails, where the scent of pine trees and the sound of rustling leaves transported me far from the bustling cities below.

Hidden Gem: San Andrés Archaeological Site

Location: La Libertad Department
Why Visit: Ancient Maya ruins with fewer crowds than Tazumal.

While Tazumal might be the more famous archaeological site, San Andrés has a charm all its own. The ruins here are smaller, but the tranquility and lack of crowds make it feel more intimate. Walking among the remnants of this ancient Maya city, I couldn't help but imagine the lives of those who once called it home.

The on-site museum was a highlight for me, with its well-preserved artifacts and informative displays about Maya culture. Unlike some of the larger sites, I felt like I had the space and time to truly connect with the history here. If you're a history buff like me, San Andrés is a gem you shouldn't miss.

Hidden Gem: Barra de Santiago

Location: Ahuachapán Department
Why Visit: A pristine estuary with rich biodiversity.

Barra de Santiago is the kind of place where you can disconnect from the world and reconnect with nature. This peaceful estuary is a haven for wildlife – from migratory birds to sea turtles. I took a boat tour through the mangroves and was amazed by the ecosystem's vibrancy.

The beaches here are also stunning, with dark volcanic sand and far fewer visitors than other coastal destinations. I stayed at a small eco-lodge where the staff were passionate about conservation. They even invited me to participate in a sea turtle release, which was an unforgettable experience.

Hidden Gem: Laguna de Alegría

Location: Alegría, Usulután Department
Why Visit: A volcanic crater lake with a mysterious emerald hue.

Laguna de Alegría, often called the "Emerald of Central America," feels like something out of a fantasy novel. The lake is nestled in a volcanic crater, and its greenish hue comes from the sulfur in its waters. Local legends say the lake is enchanted, and standing at its edge, I almost believed it.

The hike to the lake is relatively easy, and the surrounding area is perfect for a picnic or just soaking in the views. There's something magical about the stillness of the water and the way the light plays off its surface. If you're looking for a spot that's both serene and steeped in mystique, this is it.

Hidden Gem: Joya de Cerén

Location: La Libertad Department
Why Visit: A preserved Maya village frozen in time.

Known as the "Pompeii of the Americas," Joya de Cerén is a UNESCO World Heritage Site that offers an extraordinary glimpse into daily Maya life. Unlike grand ceremonial centers, this archaeological site is a snapshot of an ordinary farming village, perfectly preserved under layers of volcanic ash from a catastrophic eruption around 600 CE.

Walking through the site, I could see ancient homes, communal spaces, and even tools and food storage areas still intact. The tranquility of the area and the lack of heavy crowds made it feel like I was stepping into a hidden chapter of history. The museum nearby complements the visit, showcasing artifacts and stories that make the experience even richer.

Hidden Gem: Playa Las Flores

Location: San Miguel Department
Why Visit: A surfer's paradise with a laid-back vibe.

While most surfers flock to El Tunco, Playa Las Flores offers a quieter, more serene experience. This stretch of coastline is renowned for its consistent right-hand point breaks, making it a favorite among experienced surfers. But even if you're not into surfing, the laid-back vibe and stunning sunsets make this spot unforgettable.

The beach is less developed than other tourist areas, which adds to its charm. I stayed at a small surf lodge and spent my days alternating between swimming in the warm waters and relaxing under palm trees with a good book. The local community here is welcoming, and the slower pace of life is perfect for unwinding.

Hidden Gem: Tecapa Volcano

Location: Usulután Department
Why Visit: A coffee lover's dream with breathtaking crater views.

Tecapa Volcano isn't just a natural wonder; it's a journey into El Salvador's vibrant coffee culture. The volcano is home to lush coffee plantations, and I had the chance to visit one where the beans are grown, harvested, and roasted. The smell of fresh coffee wafting through the air as I sipped a cup overlooking the crater lake below was pure bliss.

For adventurers, there are hiking trails that lead to the top of the volcano. The views from the summit, with the emerald waters of Laguna de Alegría glimmering in the distance, were absolutely worth the effort. The blend of nature, history, and coffee made this one of my favorite hidden gems.

Hidden Gem: Perquín

Location: Morazán Department
Why Visit: A town steeped in history from the civil war era.

Perquín is a place where history comes alive. As the former headquarters of the FMLN guerrillas during El Salvador's civil war, the town is now home to the Museum of the Revolution. Walking through the museum, I saw artifacts, photographs, and even a downed helicopter that told powerful stories of resilience and struggle.

The surrounding area is equally compelling, with lush forests and waterfalls that offer a peaceful counterbalance to the town's heavy history. I also met locals who were eager to share their personal stories, making my visit feel deeply personal and enriching. Perquín isn't just a destination – it's an experience that leaves a lasting impression.

Hidden Gem: Devil's Door (La Puerta del Diablo)

Location: Panchimalco, San Salvador Department
Why Visit: Jaw-dropping rock formations and panoramic views.

La Puerta del Diablo is one of those places that takes your breath away, both literally and figuratively. This dramatic rock formation, split into two towering peaks, is steeped in legend. Locals told me stories of how it got its name, from tales of duels with the devil to its use as a hiding place during the civil war.

The hike to the top was exhilarating, with steep trails and occasional gusts of wind. Once I reached the summit, the 360-degree views were absolutely worth it. From the rolling hills to the Pacific Ocean in the distance, it felt like I was on top of the world. If you're a fan of adventure, this spot is a must.

Hidden Gem: Montecristo Cloud Forest

Location: Metapán, Santa Ana Department
Why Visit: A misty escape into lush biodiversity.

Montecristo Cloud Forest is one of the most enchanting places I've ever visited. Nestled within El Trifinio National Park, where El Salvador, Guatemala, and Honduras meet, this cloud forest is a haven for nature lovers. Walking through the misty trails felt like stepping into a dream, with orchids, ferns, and towering trees creating a magical atmosphere.

One of the highlights was reaching El Trifinio peak, where you can stand at the point where three countries converge. The cooler temperatures and abundance of bird species, including colorful quetzals, made this a refreshing escape from the heat of the lowlands. It's an unforgettable spot for anyone seeking serenity and natural beauty.

Hidden Gem: Isla Tasajera

Location: La Paz Department
Why Visit: A tranquil island with untouched beaches and mangroves.

Isla Tasajera is a small island that feels worlds away from the hustle and bustle of mainland El Salvador. I reached it by taking a boat ride through the Estero de Jaltepeque, a sprawling estuary filled with mangroves and wildlife. The journey itself was part of the adventure, with pelicans and other birds flying overhead.

On the island, life moves at a slower pace. I strolled along its pristine beaches, explored the mangroves by kayak, and even watched local fishermen bringing in their daily catch. The simplicity and authenticity of life here made it one of the most memorable parts of my trip.

Hidden Gem: Nahuizalco

Location: Sonsonate Department
Why Visit: A vibrant indigenous town with a stunning night market.

Nahuizalco is a town that truly comes alive after dark. Its famous night market is illuminated with hundreds of candles, creating a warm and inviting atmosphere. Strolling through the market, I found everything from handmade crafts to delicious street food. The smell of pupusas and freshly brewed coffee filled the air, making it impossible not to indulge.

Beyond the market, the town has a rich indigenous heritage. I visited a local cooperative where artisans showcased traditional weaving and woodwork techniques. The blend of cultural authenticity and the magical ambiance of the night market made Nahuizalco a highlight of my journey.

Hidden Gem: El Imposible National Park

Location: Ahuachapán Department
Why Visit: A rugged wilderness teeming with biodiversity.

El Imposible National Park is a paradise for hikers and nature lovers. The name itself intrigued me – it comes from the treacherous gorge that once made the area nearly impossible to access. Today, it's a protected area with miles of trails winding through dense forests, rivers, and waterfalls.

Hiking here was a true adventure. I spotted monkeys swinging through the trees, colorful butterflies flitting past, and even heard the distant calls of exotic birds. My guide shared fascinating insights about the flora and fauna, making me appreciate the park even more. It's a place where you can truly disconnect and immerse yourself in nature.

Hidden Gem: Juayúa Food Festival

Location: Juayúa, Sonsonate Department
Why Visit: A culinary celebration in a charming town.

Every weekend, the town of Juayúa hosts a food festival that's a feast for the senses. When I arrived, the streets were lined with stalls offering every kind of Salvadoran dish you could imagine – from grilled meats to tamales to decadent desserts. I tried yuca frita (fried cassava) and some of the best pupusas I've ever had.

The festival isn't just about food, though. There's live music, artisans selling handcrafted goods, and a festive atmosphere that makes you want to stay all day. Juayúa itself is a picturesque town with a stunning central plaza and the nearby Los Chorros de la Calera waterfalls, which are perfect for a post-festival adventure.

CHAPTER 6: PRACTICAL INFORMATION

Safety and Security Considerations

El Salvador is a country that carries with it a rich history, stunning natural landscapes, and a vibrancy that draws visitors looking for something unique. At the same time, it's a place where safety and security considerations often come up when you're planning your trip. Before I visited, I'd heard plenty of conflicting advice—some said it was unsafe, others insisted it was one of the most rewarding destinations in Central America. Now, having spent time exploring its cities, beaches, and mountains, I can tell you that while safety concerns are valid, they are manageable with some thoughtful preparation and a little common sense.

When I first arrived in San Salvador, the capital, I was struck by how different it was from the dramatic headlines I'd read. The city has a pulse—markets bustling with life, locals chatting at food stalls, and neighborhoods with colorful murals telling the country's story of resilience and creativity. That said, like in any urban environment, it's important to remain aware of your surroundings. I made it a habit to avoid wandering around late at night, especially in areas I wasn't familiar with. During the day, I felt comfortable exploring districts like Zona Rosa and Santa Tecla, which are known for their restaurants, cafes, and safer reputation.

Public transportation in El Salvador is an experience in itself, but it's one I approached cautiously. The brightly colored buses known as "chicken buses" are an affordable way to get around, but they can sometimes be hotspots for petty theft. I opted for ride-hailing apps like Uber or taxis arranged by my accommodation when moving around cities. It wasn't just about convenience—it gave me peace of mind knowing I was taking a safer option, especially after sunset.

Speaking of accommodations, choosing where to stay made a significant difference in how safe I felt. In urban areas, I looked for hotels or guesthouses with good reviews that specifically mentioned safety. Some places even had security guards, which is common in parts of El Salvador. In smaller towns like Suchitoto or the beachside haven of El Tunco, the vibe was more relaxed, and I felt at ease walking around even at night. Still, I always locked up my belongings and avoided leaving anything valuable in plain sight.

One of the most unforgettable parts of my trip was visiting El Salvador's natural wonders. The Ruta de las Flores, with its quaint villages and coffee plantations, felt like stepping into another world. The hike up Santa Ana Volcano, with its breathtaking views of the crater lake, was a highlight of my trip. However, I made sure to go with a guide or a group, as hiking alone in some areas can pose risks. Guides not only know the trails but also provide an added layer of security by being familiar with the region and any potential issues.

The people of El Salvador left a lasting impression on me. Everywhere I went, locals were warm, helpful, and genuinely proud of their country. However, I quickly learned that blending in was key. Flashy jewelry, expensive cameras, and even pulling out my smartphone too often could attract unwanted attention. I kept my valuables out of sight, used a discreet money belt, and carried a small amount of cash for daily expenses. This not only made me feel less like a target but also allowed me to focus on enjoying the moment.

One piece of advice I can't stress enough is the importance of staying informed. Before heading out each day, I asked locals or my accommodation staff about the areas I planned to visit. They often had up-to-date information on which neighborhoods to avoid or the best times to visit certain spots. Social media and local travel groups also became valuable resources for real-time updates on safety.

During my time in El Salvador, I noticed that the country is undergoing a transformation. The government has been making efforts to improve security, and I could see changes happening, especially in tourist-focused areas. Police and security personnel were visible in many places, particularly around popular attractions. While this presence can feel reassuring, it's always a good idea to trust your instincts. If something doesn't feel right, it's better to err on the side of caution.

Food and nightlife in El Salvador are worth mentioning because they were such a big part of my trip. Pupuserias, where you can get the iconic pupusas, were always bustling with locals and felt like safe spots to grab a meal. When it came to nightlife, I stuck to well-known venues, especially in areas like San Salvador's Zona Rosa or the laid-back beach bars in El Tunco. The energy was incredible, but I made it a point to head back to my accommodation before it got too late.

Health and emergency preparedness were also on my mind while traveling. I made sure to carry a basic first aid kit and stayed up to date on any recommended vaccinations before my trip. Drinking bottled water and avoiding raw foods in less reputable establishments helped me avoid any stomach issues. For emergencies, I saved local contact numbers, including my embassy and a few trusted taxi services, just in case.

One of the best decisions I made was purchasing travel insurance before the trip. It gave me peace of mind knowing I was covered for unexpected situations, whether it was a health issue or a stolen item. Thankfully, I didn't have to use it, but knowing it was there made me feel more secure throughout my travels.

El Salvador is a country of contrasts. There were moments of pure tranquility, like watching the sunset over the Pacific Ocean in La Libertad, and moments where I felt the need to stay extra alert, like navigating the busy streets of San Salvador. The key takeaway from my experience is that while safety concerns shouldn't be ignored, they also shouldn't deter you from exploring this incredible country. With a bit of preparation, mindfulness, and respect for local customs, El Salvador can be a deeply rewarding destination. It's a place that challenged my perceptions and left me with memories I'll treasure forever.

Money Matters and Currency Exchange

Money matters are always at the forefront of my mind when I travel, and when I visited El Salvador, it was no different. It's fascinating how money works in different countries, and El Salvador was an eye-opener for me in so many ways. Let me walk you through everything I learned about handling currency and managing money during my time there. Hopefully, my experiences will save you from the small surprises I encountered along the way.

One of the first things I noticed—and this really simplified things—was that El Salvador uses the US dollar as its official currency. This was such a relief, especially if you're coming from the States or are used to handling dollars. I didn't have to worry about exchange rates fluctuating or figuring out the value of a completely foreign currency. The ease of just pulling out a few dollars to pay for a meal, a bus ride, or a cup of coffee made the start of my trip smoother than I expected. But, as straightforward as it sounds, there were a few nuances I wasn't prepared for.

Coins, for example, caught me off guard. While paper bills are exactly what you'd find in the US, El Salvador also has its own set of coins, called centavos, which are worth fractions of a dollar. They're unique and distinctly Salvadoran, so don't be surprised if you get handed coins that look unfamiliar. At first, I kept questioning whether I'd been given the correct change, but a quick Google search confirmed that the coins were legit. It's also a good idea to keep smaller bills and coins on hand, as they're essential when paying for smaller transactions like bus fares or street food. Many vendors struggle to break large bills like $20, so having ones, fives, and tens makes life easier for everyone.

Speaking of cash, it's king in El Salvador. I had read this before going, but it really hit home when I tried to use my credit card in smaller shops and at market stalls. Most of them just don't accept cards. Even in larger establishments where cards are more common, there's often an extra charge for using them. It's one of those little fees that can add up quickly if you're not careful. So, while I usually rely on my card while traveling, I made a point of withdrawing enough cash to cover my daily expenses.

Now, withdrawing cash in El Salvador has its own quirks. ATMs are widely available in cities like San Salvador, Santa Ana, and La Libertad, but they're less common in rural areas. I remember this one instance where I was exploring Suchitoto, a charming little town, and realized I was almost out of cash. The only ATM in town was out of service, and I had to rely on the kindness of a fellow traveler who lent me a few dollars until I could find another machine. That experience taught me to always have a backup stash of cash, just in case.

Another thing about ATMs is that many of them charge a fee for withdrawals, and this can vary depending on the bank. I quickly learned to avoid using random ATMs at gas stations or convenience stores, as they had the highest fees. Instead, I stuck to machines at reputable banks, which felt more secure and had lower charges. Before withdrawing money, I also double-checked my daily withdrawal limit—something that can differ from what you're used to at home. Oh, and don't forget to notify your bank that you're traveling. I made that mistake once, and my card was temporarily blocked for "suspicious activity." Lesson learned!

Currency exchange was another aspect I didn't have to deal with much, thanks to the use of the US dollar, but I did see exchange booths at the airport and in some larger malls. These are mostly for travelers from other countries who need to convert their home currency into dollars. If you're in that boat, it's always worth comparing rates before committing to a transaction. Airport exchange booths are notorious for giving poor rates, so I'd recommend waiting until you're in the city to make the switch if you can.

As I traveled around, I noticed how much you can stretch your dollar in El Salvador. This country is surprisingly budget-friendly. Meals at local comedores, or small eateries, cost just a few dollars, and public transportation is dirt cheap. I took a colorful chicken bus for less than a dollar, and it was one of the most memorable experiences of my trip. However, if you're not used to handling cash for every little transaction, it can feel a bit old-fashioned. I found myself digging through my wallet for coins and small bills more often than I'd anticipated.

One thing I'd heard before going—and it turned out to be true—is that tipping isn't as common or expected in El Salvador as it is in other countries. In restaurants, a 10% tip is appreciated but not mandatory. That being said, I always left a little something extra if the service was exceptional. For smaller transactions, like taxi rides or street food, tipping isn't really a thing. Still, I liked rounding up as a small gesture of appreciation, especially when I saw how hard people worked.

Budgeting for my trip was another area where I learned a lot. Before arriving, I had a rough idea of what things might cost, but being on the ground gave me a clearer picture. Daily expenses can vary depending on your travel style, but even with a mid-range budget, I found I could afford a comfortable mix of activities, meals, and accommodations. For instance, a nice hotel room in San Salvador cost me around $50 a night, while budget-friendly hostels were as low as $10. Meals at mid-range restaurants rarely exceeded $10, and local buses were less than a dollar per ride. Knowing these ballpark figures helped me manage my money better and avoid unnecessary stress.

One of the highlights of my trip was visiting local markets, where bargaining is part of the experience. At first, I felt a bit awkward haggling over prices, but it quickly became fun. It's important to remember that while bargaining is expected, it should always be done respectfully. Vendors are just trying to make a living, and those few extra cents mean more to them than they do to us. My rule of thumb was to aim for a fair price without pushing too hard—usually somewhere between the initial offer and what I was willing to pay.

Safety is another topic that came up a lot before my trip. While El Salvador has made great strides in improving security, there are still areas where you need to be cautious. I was careful about where I carried my money and how I handled it in public. Instead of pulling out a wad of cash, I kept small bills in an easily accessible pocket and left larger amounts in a money belt or my hotel safe. It's a simple precaution, but it gave me peace of mind, especially in crowded places like markets and bus stations.

Digital payments and apps are starting to gain traction in El Salvador, but they're not widespread yet. I noticed a few places accepting payments through apps like PayPal or local e-wallets, but these were mostly in larger cities. If you're someone who prefers going cashless, you might find this a bit limiting. However, the introduction of Bitcoin as legal tender in El Salvador is changing the game. I saw Bitcoin ATMs in several places, and some businesses even had signs saying they accepted cryptocurrency. While I didn't use Bitcoin myself, it was fascinating to see how the country is embracing this new form of currency.

Reflecting on my time in El Salvador, I realize how much I learned about managing money in a way that felt different from other destinations. From understanding the quirks of local coins to navigating ATMs and appreciating the value of cash in a digital age, every little detail added to the richness of my experience. Traveling teaches you not just about a place but also about your own habits and adaptability. And in El Salvador, money matters were as much a part of the adventure as the stunning landscapes and warm, welcoming people.

Health Precautions

El Salvador, with its breathtaking landscapes, vibrant culture, and warm people, is a captivating destination that draws travelers from all walks of life. But, like any journey, visiting this charming Central American country requires a bit of preparation, especially when it comes to health precautions. I remember my first visit to El Salvador vividly—it was an experience packed with adventure, local flavors, and moments of awe. Along the way, though, I quickly realized that taking care of my health wasn't just about packing sunscreen or remembering my reusable water bottle. It was a matter of understanding the unique health landscape of the country.

Before setting off, I spent a fair amount of time researching vaccinations and preventative measures. Many people overlook this step, but trust me, it's worth the effort. Depending on where you're coming from, it's a good idea to ensure you're up to date on routine vaccines such as measles, mumps, and rubella (MMR), tetanus, and influenza. Additionally, vaccines for hepatitis A and typhoid are often recommended because of the risk of exposure to contaminated food or water, which can be common in some parts of the country. I also considered getting a hepatitis B vaccine since I knew I'd be spending time in remote areas and engaging in activities that might bring me into contact with local communities.

Malaria was another concern that crossed my mind. While not all regions of El Salvador are considered malaria zones, I made sure to check the specific areas I planned to visit. For travelers venturing into rural regions, it's smart to carry antimalarial medication. I personally opted for a strong insect repellent containing DEET and made a habit of applying it religiously, especially in the evenings when mosquitoes seemed most active. Lightweight, long-sleeved clothing also became my best friend—not just for mosquitoes but also for protection against the intense sun.

Speaking of the sun, let me tell you: it's no joke in El Salvador. Coming from a cooler climate, I underestimated just how intense the tropical sun could be. On my second day exploring the ruins of Joya de Cerén, I forgot to reapply sunscreen and ended up with a burn that left me regretting my oversight. Lesson learned: carry high-SPF sunscreen and a good wide-brimmed hat. Hydration is equally important, especially when trekking or exploring outdoor attractions like the volcanoes or beaches. I made it a habit to carry a reusable water bottle, but I was cautious about refilling it. Tap water in El Salvador isn't safe to drink for visitors, so I stuck to bottled or filtered water.

When it comes to food, El Salvador's cuisine is a highlight of any visit. Pupusas, the national dish, were an absolute delight—warm, cheesy, and paired with tangy curtido. But I quickly learned to be discerning about where I ate. Street food vendors were tempting, but I stuck to stalls that seemed popular and clean. If locals were lining up, that was always a good sign. Fruits and vegetables were another area of caution. I only ate peeled or thoroughly washed fruits, and when in doubt, I avoided raw salads or uncooked items.

One thing I hadn't anticipated was how important it would be to carry a small medical kit. In the back of my mind, I assumed pharmacies would be readily accessible, but that's not always the case, especially in rural areas. My kit included essentials like pain relievers, antidiarrheal medication, rehydration salts, and a basic first-aid kit with bandages and antiseptic wipes. During a hike through El Imposible National Park, I tripped on a rocky path and scraped my knee. Having those supplies on hand saved me from having to cut my adventure short to hunt for a pharmacy.

The risk of mosquito-borne illnesses like dengue fever and chikungunya was another thing I kept in mind. These diseases don't have specific vaccines or treatments, so prevention was key. Beyond wearing repellent and protective clothing, I stayed in accommodations with good mosquito netting or air conditioning to minimize the risk of bites at night. Interestingly, during my trip, I discovered that many locals use natural remedies like citronella or eucalyptus oil to repel insects, and I found these to be quite effective too.

Traveling during the COVID-19 era added another layer of preparation. While restrictions have eased considerably, I still took precautions like carrying masks and hand sanitizer. Airports and crowded public spaces, like the bustling streets of San Salvador, can be hotspots for germs. I made a point to wash my hands frequently and avoid overly crowded areas when possible.

Another health consideration I hadn't initially thought much about was altitude sickness. Parts of El Salvador, especially around its many volcanoes, are at a higher elevation than I'm used to. Although I didn't experience severe symptoms, I did notice some mild shortness of breath and fatigue during a hike up Santa Ana Volcano. To combat this, I paced myself, stayed hydrated, and took breaks as needed. If you're someone prone to altitude sickness, it might be worth consulting your doctor before heading to the higher-altitude areas.

One of the more unexpected lessons I learned was the importance of staying aware of my surroundings and maintaining a balanced diet. It's easy to get caught up in the excitement of trying new foods and forget about regular meals. On one occasion, I went nearly a whole day without eating a proper meal because I was too busy exploring the Ruta de Las Flores. By evening, I felt lightheaded and realized I hadn't consumed enough water or eaten enough to keep up with my activity level. From then on, I made it a point to pack snacks like nuts or granola bars in case I couldn't find food on the go.

Another essential part of my health strategy was travel insurance. While I didn't end up needing it, knowing I had coverage in case of an emergency gave me peace of mind. El Salvador has public and private healthcare options, but the private facilities tend to offer better services for visitors. If you're not fluent in Spanish, some private hospitals have English-speaking staff, which can be a huge relief in stressful situations.

Despite all my precautions, I did have a minor run-in with "traveler's tummy." It's one of those things that can happen no matter how careful you are. Thankfully, it wasn't severe and only lasted a day. I credited my quick recovery to staying hydrated and taking the rehydration salts I'd packed. If you do get sick while in El Salvador, don't hesitate to seek help. Pharmacies are usually well-stocked and pharmacists are often very knowledgeable.

El Salvador also has a culture of warmth and hospitality, and the locals were often eager to share their own tips for staying healthy. From recommending local remedies to pointing me toward safe eateries, their advice was invaluable. It reminded me that while preparation is crucial, being open to local knowledge can make all the difference in navigating health concerns during travel.

By the end of my trip, I realized that taking health precautions wasn't just about avoiding illness—it was about ensuring I could fully immerse myself in the beauty of El Salvador without interruptions. The vibrant sunsets over Lake Coatepeque, the exhilarating hikes through lush jungles, and the moments of connection with locals all became even more meaningful because I felt well and prepared throughout my journey.

So, if you're planning a trip to El Salvador, my advice is simple: take the time to prepare, pack smart, and listen to your body. It's a country that rewards those who venture into its landscapes and embrace its culture with open arms. By prioritizing your health, you'll be able to savor every moment and leave with memories that will stay with you long after you've returned home.

Emergency Contact Numbers in El Salvador: A Traveler's Guide with Personal Insights

When traveling to El Salvador, the tropical landscapes, vibrant culture, and warm locals will captivate you. But as any seasoned traveler will tell you, being prepared for the unexpected is just as important as packing your sunscreen. During my time exploring El Salvador, I found it essential to keep a list of emergency contact numbers handy. From natural disasters to minor inconveniences, a quick response can make all the difference.

In this guide, I'll share practical advice on how to access emergency services in El Salvador, including personal anecdotes and tips to help you navigate the country safely and confidently.

General Emergency Services in El Salvador

911 – The National Emergency Line

El Salvador's 911 service covers police, medical, and fire emergencies. While it's modeled after the system in the U.S., I found it reassuring that operators can sometimes assist in English. However, Spanish remains the primary language, so brushing up on key phrases or having a translation app can help.

One memorable moment during my trip was when a fellow traveler needed urgent medical attention in San Salvador. We called 911, and within minutes, an ambulance was on its way. The system might not be perfect, especially in remote areas, but in cities like San Salvador and Santa Ana, it's relatively reliable.

Medical Emergencies

Hospital Emergency Services

If you find yourself needing medical assistance, it's good to know which hospitals to contact. Public hospitals provide free emergency care, but private hospitals are often better equipped and faster.

- **Hospital Nacional Rosales (Public)**
  Address: Avenida Independencia, San Salvador
  Phone: +503 2231-9200
  Tip: Public hospitals can be crowded. If time is of the essence, consider a private clinic.
- **Hospital de Diagnóstico (Private)**
  Address: Paseo General Escalón, San Salvador
  Phone: +503 2505-5000
  Tip: This hospital was a lifesaver for a friend of mine who needed stitches after a hiking trip. It's clean, efficient, and has English-speaking staff.

Red Cross El Salvador

The Salvadoran Red Cross provides emergency medical care, disaster relief, and ambulance services.

- **Phone:** +503 2222-5155
  The Red Cross helped me navigate a minor food allergy incident. The team was professional and quick, even though it was late at night.

Police Assistance

National Civil Police (Policía Nacional Civil - PNC)

The National Civil Police is your go-to for reporting crimes or suspicious activities. Unfortunately, petty theft is not uncommon in busy tourist areas, so having this number saved can be useful.

- **Emergency Line:** 911
- **Tourist Police (Politur):** +503 2511-8300

I once needed Politur's assistance after losing my wallet in La Libertad. They were incredibly kind and spoke enough English to guide me through filing a report. The tourist police are trained specifically to assist visitors, so don't hesitate to contact them.

Fire Emergencies

National Fire Department (Cuerpo de Bomberos Nacionales)

While El Salvador doesn't experience massive wildfires, localized fires can still occur. Whether it's a kitchen fire in your Airbnb or something more serious, the firefighters are well-trained and quick to respond.

- **Emergency Line:** 911
- **Direct Contact:** +503 2527-7300

During my stay in Santa Ana, I witnessed a small fire in a market. The response time was impressive, and the fire department handled the situation efficiently.

Roadside Assistance

Automóvil Club de El Salvador (ACES)

Driving in El Salvador can be an adventure, with potholes and unpredictable traffic. If you're renting a car and face a breakdown, ACES provides roadside assistance.

- **Phone:** +503 2133-9100
  I relied on ACES when my rental car got a flat tire near Suchitoto. They arrived within 45 minutes and even helped with directions afterward.

Transportation Accidents

For accidents involving multiple vehicles or injuries, you'll need to involve the police and possibly your insurance company. The general advice is to remain at the scene and call 911 or the PNC.

Natural Disasters

Ministry of Environment and Natural Resources (MARN)

El Salvador is prone to earthquakes, volcanic activity, and tropical storms. Staying informed can make a huge difference.

- **Phone:** +503 2132-6400
- **Website:** www.marn.gob.sv

I experienced a mild earthquake during my trip and was impressed by the local disaster management system. MARN's updates were prompt, and they provided clear safety instructions via text alerts.

Embassies and Consulates

U.S. Embassy in El Salvador

- **Address:** Final Boulevard Santa Elena, Antiguo Cuscatlán
- **Phone:** +503 2501-2999
- **Emergency After-Hours:** +503 2501-2000

The U.S. Embassy was a reliable point of contact when I lost my passport. They expedited the process and even gave tips on staying safe while waiting for a replacement.

Other Embassies

If you're not a U.S. citizen, it's wise to locate your country's embassy or consulate. Most embassies in San Salvador offer emergency assistance for their nationals.

Practical Tips for Emergencies

1. **Save Numbers Before Arrival**
   Before you land, program these emergency contacts into your phone. Include both local numbers and your home country's consulate.
2. **Carry a Portable Charger**
   In emergencies, a dead phone is the last thing you want. I learned this the hard way while hiking in El Imposible National Park.
3. **Download Offline Maps**
   Google Maps offline mode was a game-changer for me. It helped me locate hospitals and police stations even without internet access.
4. **Learn Basic Spanish**
   Knowing how to say "help" (ayuda) or "emergency"

(emergencia) can go a long way. During my trip, locals were always willing to assist but often spoke little English.
5. **Get Travel Insurance**
Travel insurance is your safety net. Whether it's covering medical expenses or lost luggage, it's worth the investment.

Transportation & Getting Around in El Salvador: A Personal Guide

When visiting El Salvador, getting around might seem a bit daunting at first. It's a small yet incredibly vibrant country with diverse landscapes, from bustling cities to serene beaches and lush mountains. Having explored the country myself, I can assure you that once you grasp the local transportation system, traveling becomes a part of the adventure. Here's everything you need to know to navigate El Salvador with confidence.

Public Buses: The Heartbeat of El Salvador's Transport System

One of the most iconic ways to travel around El Salvador is by public buses. Known locally as **"chicken buses"**, these vehicles are repurposed American school buses decked out with colorful paint, loud music, and sometimes flashing lights. Riding these buses is an experience in itself—you feel the pulse of Salvadoran life as locals hop on and off, vendors sell snacks and drinks, and vibrant reggaetón blares from the speakers.

Routes:
Public buses cover almost every corner of the country. For instance:

- **Route 201**: This popular route connects San Salvador to Santa Ana, passing through charming towns like El Congo.
- **Route 102**: If you're heading to the beaches in La Libertad, this is your go-to bus.
- **Inter-city buses**: There are direct services between major hubs like San Salvador, San Miguel, and Ahuachapán.

The routes can feel a bit overwhelming at first since there's no centralized app or website for schedules. But locals are friendly and usually more than happy to point you in the right direction.

Fare:
Public buses are incredibly cheap. A ride on a local bus costs anywhere from **$0.20 to $0.35**, while longer distances might set you back about **$1–$2**. Carry small bills, as drivers rarely have change for large denominations.

Operating Hours:
Most buses operate from **5:00 AM to 8:00 PM**, but it's best to finish your journey before nightfall for safety reasons.

Tips:
If you're new to the chicken bus experience, try to sit near the front for a smoother ride and fewer vendor interruptions. Also, hold on tight—drivers often take sharp turns with a certain…enthusiasm.

Microbuses: Fast and Convenient

Microbuses are smaller, privately operated vans that run on fixed routes. These are faster than public buses and make fewer stops, which makes them ideal for travelers who are short on time.

Routes:
They cover similar routes as the larger buses but are especially

common on busy city routes like **San Salvador to Santa Tecla** or **Soyapango**.

Fare:
The fares for microbuses are slightly higher, usually around **$0.30 to $0.50** for short distances and up to **$2 for longer trips**.

Operating Hours:
These generally follow the same schedule as public buses, running from early morning to evening.

Card/Token System:
Microbuses, like the chicken buses, operate on a cash-only basis. Make sure you have exact change to avoid delays.

My Take:
I loved taking microbuses because they're quicker and less crowded. However, they can be a tight squeeze if you're carrying a lot of luggage.

Taxis: Convenient but Costly

Taxis in El Salvador are everywhere, especially in urban areas like San Salvador. While they offer door-to-door convenience, they're generally more expensive than other forms of transportation.

Fare:
Fares vary depending on the city and distance, but a short ride within San Salvador might cost **$5–$10**, while longer trips can climb to **$20–$30**. Unfortunately, meters are rare, so it's essential to negotiate the price upfront.

Tips:

- Stick to **authorized taxis**, which are usually white with a taxi sign.
- Avoid hailing taxis on the street late at night. Instead, ask your hotel or restaurant to call a trusted taxi company.

My Advice:
While taxis are convenient, I found ride-sharing apps like Uber to be a safer and more cost-effective option, especially in cities.

Ride-Sharing Apps: A Game-Changer

If you're not up for haggling with taxi drivers, ride-sharing apps like **Uber** and **InDriver** are lifesavers. They're widely available in cities like San Salvador, Santa Tecla, and San Miguel.

Fare:
Uber fares are generally reasonable, with short trips costing around **$3–$5**. Longer trips, such as a ride to El Tunco beach, might cost **$15–$25**.

Operating Hours:
Uber operates 24/7, making it a reliable option for late-night outings.

Why I Recommend It:
I relied heavily on Uber during my visit, especially when traveling at night or to less familiar areas. The convenience of cashless payment and GPS tracking made it a hassle-free experience.

Renting a Car: Freedom to Explore

For those who prefer to explore at their own pace, renting a car is an excellent option. El Salvador's roads are generally well-maintained, and the country is small enough that you can drive from one end to the other in just a few hours.

Cost:
Car rentals start at about **$30–$50 per day**, plus the cost of fuel, which is around **$4–$5 per gallon**. Be sure to factor in toll fees, especially on major highways.

Tips for Drivers:

- Traffic can be chaotic in cities, so patience is key.
- Watch out for pedestrians and motorcycles, which often weave through traffic unexpectedly.
- If you're driving to rural areas, a **4x4 vehicle** might be necessary, especially during the rainy season.

Why I Loved Driving:
Driving gave me the flexibility to visit off-the-beaten-path gems like **Suchitoto** and the **Ruta de las Flores** at my own pace. The scenic drives alone are worth it!

Intercity Buses: Comfort for Long Distances

If you're planning to travel between cities, consider using the more comfortable intercity buses, such as **Ticabus** or **King Quality**. These buses are a far cry from the bustling chicken buses—they're air-conditioned, have reclining seats, and sometimes even Wi-Fi.

Routes:

- **Ticabus** connects San Salvador with neighboring countries like Guatemala, Honduras, and Nicaragua.
- **King Quality** offers routes to major Salvadoran cities like San Miguel and Santa Ana.

Fare:
Tickets range from **$10 to $30**, depending on the destination and class of service.

Operating Hours:
Schedules vary, but most services operate during the day. It's best to book tickets in advance to secure your spot.

Why It's Worth It:
I took Ticabus from San Salvador to Guatemala City, and the journey was smooth and stress-free. It's perfect for travelers who prefer comfort over the rustic charm of chicken buses.

Boats and Ferries: Exploring Coastal Routes

For water enthusiasts, boat and ferry services offer a unique way to explore El Salvador's stunning coastline and inland lakes.

Routes:

- **La Unión Ferry** connects El Salvador to Nicaragua via the Gulf of Fonseca.
- Small boats operate in places like **Lago de Coatepeque**, offering short scenic rides.

Fare:
Prices vary widely, but expect to pay around **$10–$30** for boat rides.

Why I Loved It:
The boat ride on Lago de Coatepeque was one of the highlights of my trip. The turquoise waters and surrounding volcanoes create an unforgettable backdrop.

Cycling: A Fun Alternative

If you're an active traveler, cycling is an enjoyable way to explore smaller towns and rural areas. Cities like Santa Tecla have bike-friendly streets, and some hostels and tour operators rent bikes for about **$10–$15 per day**.

Tips:
Stick to designated bike paths when possible, and avoid cycling on busy highways. Morning rides are best, as the heat can be intense later in the day.

Why It's Memorable:
Cycling through the coffee plantations in the mountains of El Salvador was a dream. The fresh air and breathtaking views made every uphill climb worth it.

Printed in Great Britain
by Amazon